EVERGLADES

THE PARK STORY

By William B. Robertson, Jr.,
Senior Park Biologist

Photography By Glenn Van Nimwegen

As well as I can remember, I wrote the original draft of "Everglades —The Park Story" in two or three hectic weeks during the summer of 1958. Dan Beard said he wanted a park book and one didn't like to keep him waiting. After the customary editorial agonies, the book appeared a year or so later, suitably clothed in Dade Thornton's fine photographs. At that time it cost a mere buck and it stayed in print for nearly 20 years, while south Florida changed around it.

Looking back from 1988, those days seem unimaginably remote. The park was still in its age of innocence: small staff, not much money, 20-horsepower outboards, few visitors. Specialization was a luxury we couldn't afford and serendipity lived.

There was an archaic and unprogrammed zest just to explore the place. To find an unknown Indian mound, a lost hammock, a different way to get from here to there. The new park road was building, but part of the way to Flamingo still followed the narrow, chuck-holed, unforgiving stretches of the Old Ingraham Highway. The Central and Southern Florida Flood Control Project edged ever closer, but it was something that was happening up north. In the park, the glades still flooded or they didn't flood, an act of God and that was that. Code words for water delivery structures like L-29, S-12 and C-111 hadn't yet entered our lexicon. Our concerns about park resources were simple and direct — alligator poaching, theft of tree snails and orchids, turtle-turning on Cape Sable beaches, fighting fires we probably should have ignored. Few Florida biologists had ever heard of such introduced

pests as Brazilian pepper or Melaleuca or walking catfish. A few months earlier, the park had done a landmark first prescribed burn and the debate still raged, longer and hotter than the fire. Hurricane Donna, the Hole-in-the-Donut, official lists of endangered species, the Big Cypress Jetport, the minimum water-delivery schedule, the Frog Pond...were still in our future. How little we knew. How quickly it all changed.

Preparing a second edition forced me to re-read "The Park Story" for the first time in many years. Hundreds of small changes had to be made to take note of new information, to beef up lamentably weak sections, and to smooth the too-numerous patches of awkward writing.

Daniel Beard first Superintendent of Everglades National Park.

Overall, however, it was encouraging that so much of the text could stand more or less as written. I take that to mean that the fundamentals of the park remained largely intact, while the world around us changed at breakneck speed into something scarcely recognizable to a time traveler from the south Florida of the 1950s. I suppose that's the essence of conservation and National Parks. Let us hope that the park continues relatively unscathed through the next several decades of testing confrontations and final adjustments. Then, when someone else sits down to write a better "Park Story" after a while, he can still speak of wood storks and panthers and everything else that makes southern Florida wildlands such a glory to behold.

Homestead, FL
July 10, 1988

CONTENTS

ABOVE *Islands of forest occupy slight rises of ground in the broad vista of sawgrass.*

INSET *Stunted by fire and shallow soil, this dwarf cypress may be more than 100 years old.*

THE

CHAPTER ONE

EVERGLADES LANDSCAPE

Everglades National Park preserves a unique American landscape where the temperate zone meets the subtropics, blending the wildlife and vegetation of both. Perhaps it is also not quite what many visitors expect to find. Instead of tropical profusion, the first impression is boundless space of marsh, water and sky. Closer inspection reveals scenes of strange wilderness beauty...the palm-tufted hammocks where the sawgrass meets the mangroves; the clean, lonely sweep of the Cape Sable beaches; the Gulf Coast rivers, dark tide-ways threading the ancient mangrove forest; the many-colored waters of Florida Bay where, on summer days of dead calm the blue of sky and sea are one, the horizon line is lost and distant islands seem to hang in mid-air.

Yet, the Everglades is a different sort of place than most visitors have seen and it takes some getting used to. Especially so because one usually reaches the Everglades by crossing wide developed areas where the natural landscape has been almost totally obliterated. This book aims to smooth the introduction without trespassing too heavily on the right of each newcomer to discover the Everglades for himself. It attempts merely to set the stage, to provide a context that may help the visitor to better understand his own discoveries.

An old story (if it isn't true, it deserves to be) tells of a cowboy who at his first sight of the Grand Canyon exclaimed with deep conviction: "Something sure did happen here." In contrast, one viewing the horizon-wide level of the Everglades might conclude with some justice that nothing much had happened there. If a landscape needs mountains to qualify as scenery, then South Florida is supremely unscenic, because few places are flatter. The park's highest point attains a dizzy altitude of about 10 feet above sea level. Flatness is so fundamental a characteristic of the country that we may well take a look into the geological past to see how it came about.

Florida's ultimate foundation is a feature geologists call the Floridian Plateau, a flat-topped elevated area projecting southward from the continent between the deep basins of the Atlantic Ocean and the Gulf of Mexico. The core of the 300-mile wide Plateau is made up of volcanic and altered rocks, and its edges are steep, descending abruptly to the ocean depths. This evidence of ancient volcanic activity and folding suggests

that at one time things indeed were happening. That time, however, is remote. For many millions of years Florida has been one of the most stable parts of the earth's thin crust. Its more recent geological history records only the rise and fall of the sea upon a quiescent land mass. The Floridian may again find salt water lapping round his ankles, but he rests in little danger of earthquakes.

Throughout its geological existence Florida has alternately been submerged and then exposed beyond its present shores, because of changes in sea level. During the times when the sea covered the land there was a constant deposit of sediments on the bottom. When the sea withdrew, some of the deposits were removed by erosion. Through many repetitions of this cycle, more sediment was left during the periods of

flooding than was washed away during the sea's retreat, so that a great depth of limestone and other sedimentary layers was gradually built up over the old basement rocks. In southern Florida the sedimentary blanket is more than three miles thick. The various layers lie almost level, just as they were deposited. Wherever erosion carved valleys or

ABOVE *Elevation*
change of a few
inches marks the
boundary between
pine and saw
grass.
INSET *Intricate,*
endless mangrove
waterways make
up much of the
coastal area.

sink holes at the times when Florida was above water, these irregularities were more or less smoothed during the next interval of flooding. The country's present flatness reflects the fact that through most of its days it has been covered by a shallow sea.

The ebb and flow of sea level that had most to do with determining present topography occurred during the Pleistocene ice ages, quite recently as geologists reckon time. In this period, continental glaciers made five major advances and each ice age was followed by a warmer interglacial period. No icebergs floated in Biscayne Bay (though some northern species of plants and animals found refuge in Florida), but the glacial sequence was important, because it caused great changes in sea level.

As the glaciers grew they sucked up the seas, and as they

melted, the seas rose again over Florida. The earlier sea invasions deeply submerged southern Florida (of the whole peninsula little remained above water except the tops of a few central Florida sand hills) and left no recognizable sediments.

The third interglacial sea, about 100,000 years ago, deposited the limestone beds that now occur near the surface over much of South Florida. One of these formations, called the Key Largo Limestone, is an old coral reef that today forms the Upper Florida Keys from Biscayne National Park southward past Marathon. Another, the Miami Limestone, makes up the east coast ridge on the mainland, dips to provide a floor for the southern Everglades and Florida Bay, and emerges again forming the islands from the neighborhood of Big Pine Key to beyond Key West.

After these limestone formations had been deposited, another glacier pushed down into the northern United States. Sea levels fell, Florida was exposed far beyond its present shoreline, and the soft surface limestones were subjected to erosion. After this glacier retreated, Florida again was flooded briefly to a point 25 feet above present sea level, much less than in former interglacial periods but deep enough to submerge most of South Florida. Then the whole glacial cycle was repeated one more time, with ice advance and lowered sea level, ice retreat and rising

seas. That brings us at last to the present day and to Florida's present shape on the map.

It may also bring us to the uneasy question, "What's happening to sea level right now?" Well, most evidence seems to say that the sea is rising, just as if we were experiencing still another interglacial period. Studies of buried peat deposits suggest that the present rise has been in progress for at least 14,000 years at rates that have varied from one and a half to five inches per century. Those may seem like trivial amounts, but along the flat coast of South Florida the effects are quickly evident. Comparison of early and recent aerial photographs shows that mangrove-bordered streams along the park's southwest coast have extended inland measurably in a mere 40 years. Also, it is feared that the rate of sea-level rise may be increasing because gasses from worldwide burning of oil and coal have changed the atmosphere in ways that lead to warmer climate, the so-called "greenhouse effect." We are certain to hear much more about rising sea level and Everglades National Park is likely to be one of the first places where, a century or so hence, the effects of the rising sea become obvious and inescapable.

With some assurance, at least, that the sea will not be upon us this week or next, we may look briefly at the shape of land which resulted from the long, quiet geological processes that built South Florida. Having said at length that the country is

flat, it is now necessary to point out that it is not completely so, and that the small variations from absolute level play a major role in determining the landscape.

A surface profile across South Florida would look something like the cross-section of a shallow saucer. Although the whole region is an extremely flat plain lying nearly at sea level, the land along both coasts is slightly more elevated. To the east is an eroded limestone ridge formed by outcrops of the Miami Limestone. It extends along the coast from north of Fort Lauderdale to Florida City and thence far west into the park. On the west side of the peninsula, there is no definite ridge but a wide area of somewhat higher land. These higher areas partially enclose an interior basin that is now occupied by the Everglades. The South Florida saucer is tilted almost imperceptibly toward the south and west, with an average seaward slope of no more than a few inches to the mile, and there is a wide break in the rim at the southwest side along the Gulf of Mexico.

To make an Everglades in this enclosed level area, two more things were required—water, and a covering impervious enough to keep the water from escaping into the porous underlying limestone. There was plenty of water. Rainfall amounted to about 50 inches a year. In addition, the natural drainage of a large area in central Florida flowed into Lake Okeechobee and in flood seasons moved seaward by spilling over the low south shore of the lake. The calking–which allows some seepage but not drainage–was provided in the past few thousand years by marl deposited on top of the limestone and reinforced later by peat deposits laid down by sawgrass and other marsh plants.

Thus, the scene was set, and the Everglades developed, occupying most of the width of southern Florida, a shallow marshy river whose waters drifted slowly southward for 120 miles from Lake Okeechobee to the sea. The Seminoles called it "Pahay-okee," grassy waters. It is the dominant feature of south Florida landscape, and other parts of the scene must be understood in relation to it.

The very flatness of the Everglades area gives heightened importance to minor topographic variations. Sites that differ in elevation by no more than a few inches may present altogether different conditions for plant growth, and on the subdued topography of South Florida varying plant cover provides most of the variety in the landscape. Discussion of Everglades National Park scenery soon becomes an account of the different kinds of vegetation and the natural forces that govern their occurrence. For present purposes we may distinguish five types–hammocks, bayheads, pineland, mangrove swamps and the sawgrass Everglades. It is convenient to separate these into upland and lowland divisions, always remembering that the differences in elevation are on a Lilliputian scale.

Mangrove swamps and sawgrass marshes occur on land which is normally overflowed during at least part of the year. The sawgrass prairies of the Everglades take up the interior fresh water sections, and near the coasts are replaced by mangrove swamps. Together, sawgrass and mangrove cover most of the park area. Wherever some other kind of vegetation is found, a difference in land elevation is to be suspected.

When a South Floridian speaks of "the Glades" he means the sawgrass country. Wide vistas of sawgrass with scattered islands of trees constitute most of the interior scenery of the park. These open marshes are flooded during the summer rainy season, dry and sometimes swept by fire in late winter and spring. Here and there over the glades are ponds and deeper channels that hold permanent water except in the driest years. The smaller pools are often called "gator holes" (they resemble, and often are, the ponds maintained by large alligators) while the larger drainage channels are "sloughs" or "slough runs." Taylor Slough, where Anhinga Trail is located, is a good example. The sloughs and gator holes provide dry season refuges for the small fish, snails and crayfish of the glades, and they are often focal points for winter concentrations of alligators, birds and mammals that feed on this aquatic life.

The mangrove swamps of South Florida shores provide some of the area's strangest scenery. The views of arching roots, somber brown pools and tangled depths convey more than a suggestion of dark secrets unyielded. This forest that thrives in areas flooded by the tide and in saline soil near the coast, and even goes to sea by establishing seedlings in open water, is something altogether new to most visitors. A broad belt of mangrove swamp covers most of the coastline and extends inland to meet the sawgrass. Closely similar forests are found along ocean shores throughout the tropics. On the remote west coast of the park where the intricately braided channels of Shark River enter the Gulf of Mexico, stands one of the largest and best developed mangrove forests on earth. Or, more correctly, such a forest stood there before hurricane Donna swept the area in September, 1960, with sustained winds of 180 miles per hour. Donna left a path of desolation several miles wide along the entire Gulf Coast of the park. Most of the large mangroves were left as standing dead snags, stripped of twigs and branches. At the time, it was hard to believe that the area could recover, but, 30 years later, it is clothed with a vigorous young mangrove forest, studded here and there

with giant trees that survived the storm.

Three kinds of forest vegetation–pine woods, hammocks and bayheads–occupy the higher land around the edges of the glades and within the Everglades basin. These types of plant cover take up much less area than either sawgrass or mangrove, but each is an important element in the regional landscape.

Throughout the coastal plain of the southeastern United States, piney woods are a prominent part of the scene and the pines grow chiefly in flat, sandy areas. Visitors driving down the Florida Peninsula will traverse miles of such country, commonly called "pine flatwoods." But, as is the case with many things, the pine woods of far southern Florida are something a little different. Here pines are found only in elevated areas of bare rock where the Miami Limestone outcrops. We do not ordinarily think of pine forest as tropical vegetation, but the only plant community closely resembling the South Florida pine rockland is the so-called "pineyard" of the northern Bahamas. Frequent fires in these peculiar pinelands leave little ground cover, and the trees seem to spring from solid rock. Closer examination will show that the limestone surface is riddled with solution holes containing small pockets of soil where the pines are rooted.

Originally, pine forest covered most of the limestone ridge along the southeast coast of Florida, and also several of the Lower Florida Keys. The mainland pine ridge was a favored hunting ground of the Indians and other early settlers. Later, the extremely hard and termite-resistant wood of the "Dade County Pine" formed the basis of an important lumbering industry, and a number of communities in the area began as lumber towns in the early 1900s.

In more recent years, the South Florida pine forest has been disappearing at a steadily accelerating rate to make way for housing and farming. Pineland is high land in a region where elevation is a scarce commodity, and this characteristic has sealed its fate. No great power of prophecy is needed to foresee the time when Long Pine Key in the park will be the only sizable area of pine that remains in the South Florida landscape.

The "hammocks" of Everglades National Park are not the sort meant for lounging. Rather, they are a major feature of the vegetation, and this unexpected usage of a familiar word often gives the visitor difficulty. What is a hammock? The term is used in the southeastern United States to refer to certain kinds of mature hardwood forests. More exact definition becomes troublesome, because usage has varied with different writers and in different localities. In South Florida, the name hammock is applied to forests containing a great variety of broad-leaved trees and shrubs most of which are of West

ABOVE *Royal palm trees tower above a hammock and the adjoining sawgrass slough. The flooded slough helps protect the forest from fire.*
LEFT *The wood stork can obtain enough food to raise young only if fish are densely concentrated.*

11

Indian origin. Seeds of these plants originally drifted to our shores in the currents of the Gulf Stream or were carried from the Antilles by hurricanes and by migrating birds.

The hammocks of the Florida Keys and the south coast closely resemble forests found near the coasts of Cuba and the Bahamas. Farther inland away from the warming effects of the sea, a few northern trees, such as hackberry and red mulberry, grow in hammocks with the tropical species. Where rainfall is high, as at Paradise Key and Mahogany Hammock, the hammocks are dense, moist forests, rich in mosses and ferns. Here the trees grow large, and epiphytic orchids, ferns and bromeliads form aerial gardens along their branches. Southwestward toward Cape Sable and out along the Florida Keys, the appearance of the hammocks reflects the lower rainfall. Here the trees are smaller and more of them drop their leaves during the winter dry season. The forests are more open and air plants fewer.

Hammocks are found in South Florida as islands of dense jungle in the open pine woods, at a few places out in the Everglades, and along parts of the coast. Two things may at once be said of any place where they occur. The site is so high that it is seldom flooded, and it has enjoyed some natural protection from fire. Hammock plants tend to occupy all raised surfaces of the land–natural elevations of a foot or two, like the

limestone outcrops and the shell beaches and marl ridges along the coast, and man-made rises like the mounds of the early Indians and the embankments of modern roads. Fire presents a check to this tendency, so that hammocks are not likely to develop to maturity except at spots that have some fire protection. As Royal Palm painfully illustrates, fire also endangers long-established hammocks in years of severe drought.

Hundreds of tree islands dot the marshy expanses of the Everglades. In South Florida parlance, they go by such names as "bayhead," "cypress head" and "willow head," the terms indicating isolated stands of these trees in the open glades. The taller trees usually stand in the center, giving the island a humped or dome shape. The tree islands appear to mark the location of small topographic variations on the general level of the sawgrass plain. Bayheads are usually found on slight elevations of peat soil; cypress heads usually occupy shallow ponds. Most of the tree islands to be seen in the park are bayheads, low tangled forests much overgrown with vines. In contrast to the hammocks, bayheads have only a few kinds of trees, principally species of bay, magnolia and holly common in swamp forests throughout the southern states. The peat soil of the bayheads burns readily when it is dry, and glades fires in very dry years may completely remove bayheads from the landscape or perhaps leave a circle of dead trees to mark the former site.

A great many environmental forces affect the occurrence of the various types of plant cover and thus take a hand in shaping the landscape. As we have seen, the Everglades is a land of paradoxes. Fire is a major influence in country much of which is flooded for half the year. Elevation is a critical factor in a region flatter than most pancakes. Inland penetration of salt water, hurricanes and occasional spells of freezing weather have all played a role in determining the pattern of natural vegetation seen today. This pattern may seem at first sight to have little rhyme or reason, but actually it is the outcome of the long interaction of vegetation and environment. The hammocks of Long Pine Key, for example, continually encroach upon the pineland; and, just as steadily, fire has acted to check their advance and to maintain the more fire-adapted pine woods. Long opposition to forces in many such instances has resulted in a sort of dynamic balance, where essential stability of vegetation is achieved by means of constant small adjustments. The present scenery of Everglades National Park represents the equilibrium reached.

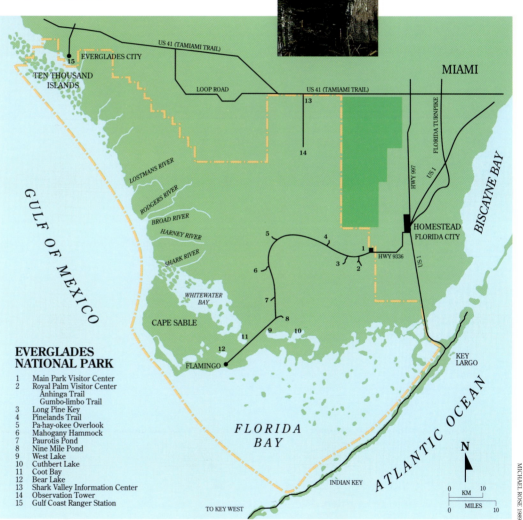

ABOVE *In very dry years, saw-grass fires like this one might be damaging, but they play an important role in maintaining the Everglades land-scape.*

INSET *Cypress trees often are hosts for bromeli-ads and other epiphytic plants.*

US 41 (TAMIAMI TRAIL)

EVERGLADES CITY

TEN THOUSAND ISLANDS

LOOP ROAD

US 41 (TAMIAMI TRAIL)

MIAMI

13

14

FLORIDA TURNPIKE

HWY 997

US 1

BISCAYNE BAY

LOSTMANS RIVER

RODGERS RIVER

BROAD RIVER

HARNEY RIVER

SHARK RIVER

GULF OF MEXICO

HOMESTEAD FLORIDA CITY

1 HWY 9336

US 1

5

4

6

3 2

WHITEWATER BAY

7

CAPE SABLE

8

9 10

KEY LARGO

11

12

FLAMINGO

EVERGLADES NATIONAL PARK

1 Main Park Visitor Center
2 Royal Palm Visitor Center
   Anhinga Trail
   Gumbo-limbo Trail
3 Long Pine Key
4 Pinelands Trail
5 Pa-hay-okee Overlook
6 Mahogany Hammock
7 Paurotis Pond
8 Nine Mile Pond
9 West Lake
10 Cuthbert Lake
11 Coot Bay
12 Bear Lake
13 Shark Valley Information Center
14 Observation Tower
15 Gulf Coast Ranger Station

FLORIDA BAY

ATLANTIC OCEAN

N

INDIAN KEY

0 KM 10

MILES

0 10

TO KEY WEST

 Area to be added by pending legislation to expand the northeast boundary area of Everglades National Park. The expansion will enable water to flow through the park in a more natural pattern.

THE
NATURAL HISTORY

Wildlife is the part of the Everglades National Park scene that attracts most attention from visitors. A great variety of rare and unusual plants and animals and impressive spectacles of wildlife abundance, all in a setting exhibiting strong touches of the tropics, make the park a showplace of natural history.

Part of the charm of the area for the biologist lies in the fact that there are still new things to be discovered and important observations yet to be made. Before presenting a much abbreviated roll call of the park's wildlife, it may be well to notice several characteristics that have had great influence in determining the kinds of plants and animals found in South Florida.

Visitors to the park are sometimes concerned to know whether the area is, as they say, "really tropical." This question is far too complicated for a simple yes-or-no answer. The various lines of evidence are somewhat contradictory.

In a strictly geographical sense, South Florida narrowly misses the tropics. The southernmost land in the Florida Keys is some 75 miles north of the Tropic of Cancer, by definition the northern boundary of the Tropical Zone. The Tropic of Cancer, however, is just a straight line around the globe, and nature is seldom governed by straight lines. Another characteristic of areas in the tropics (aside from high mountains) is that they are free from frost. Here too, southernmost Florida is not quite tropical, because winter cold fronts–Yankee weather–often bring light frost to low-lying spots in the interior, and, occasionally, freezes severe enough to damage crops and kill native plants and animals that are most susceptible to cold.

Opposed to these considerations is the fact that the plant and animal life of southern Florida and its surrounding waters is in many respects exceedingly similar to that of nearby areas in the West Indies. When one thinks of such things as the mangrove swamps and coral reefs, it is easy to regard South Florida as simply another West Indian island that happens to be connected to the continental mainland. Some biologists have considered the similarities strong enough to rate the area as tropical; others take a more cautious approach and call it subtropical.

In reality, there is no place where one can draw a line and say: "Everything on this side is tropical, and all on that side belongs to temperate climes." Instead, there is a broad zone embracing much of peninsular Florida, where tropical forms mingle with those from farther north. Tropical influences are more evident near the coast than in the interior, and, of course, they become more marked as one proceeds southward in Florida. By the time the latitude of Miami is reached, a large proportion of the plants and animals which link the area to the rest of the mainland

United States have been left behind. If it is not to be termed "truly tropical," Everglades National Park at least represents the threshold of the Antillean tropics, and the door is broadly ajar.

One reason for a difference of opinion among biologists is that some groups of plants and animals in South Florida include many tropical forms, while others have few or none. In general, the environmental setting is distinctly West Indian, but most of the larger land animals are not tropical species. Dr. Frank Chapman, the renowned ornithologist, once remarked that one expected to see parrots and toucans in the profusion of tropical growth at Royal Palm, and instead saw cardinals and mockingbirds. Perhaps an added example will clarify this point.

In the course of a walk through a hammock in the park, one might observe, say, a raccoon, a blue jay and a black snake–nothing especially tropical about any of these creatures; they could be seen as readily in Illinois or Connecticut. However, the tree the raccoon climbs, the insect the blue jay catches and the lizard that the black snake has just eaten are likely to be tropical species not found elsewhere in the United States. Explanation of this necessitates a short excursion into biogeography, the division of biological science which strives to understand why the various kinds of plants and animals occur where they do.

The two important biogeographical points are: First, South Florida provides climatic conditions suitable for many West Indian plants and animals; and, second, Florida, through all the ups and downs of its geological history, has never had a land connection with any area in the West Indies, but has frequently been attached to the continental mainland, as it is today. In other words, South Florida has been a place where West Indian forms might thrive, provided they were able to get there, and an area continental forms were easily able to reach, provided they could live successfully in the near-tropical climate. As a consequence of this rather unusual state of affairs, the present natural life of South Florida is a mixed assortment of tropical West Indian species and northern continental species.

CROSS SECTION OF THE EVERGLADES

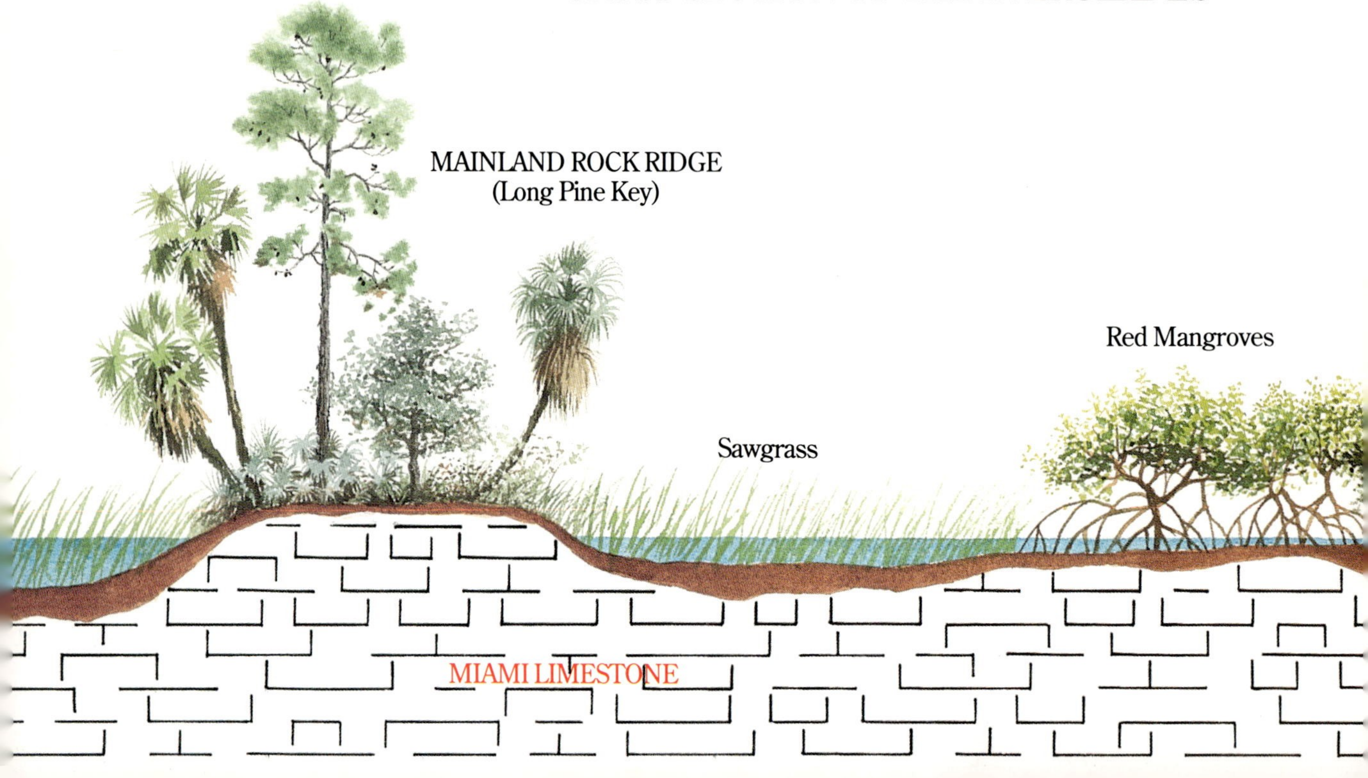

MAINLAND ROCK RIDGE
(Long Pine Key)

Red Mangroves

Sawgrass

MIAMI LIMESTONE

For almost every sort of marine life, the water gap that separates the tip of Florida from the West Indies is no barrier, but rather an open highway. Thus it is that the plants and animals of the shores and shallow coastal waters of South Florida are often almost identical with those found in similar situations throughout the Caribbean. In general, South Florida has the same kinds of marine mammals, water birds, sea turtles, and salt water fish–not to mention a host of other marine animals, such as sea shells and corals, and a great variety of marine plants. In many of these groups, a sprinkling of northern forms also reaches South Florida, and as a result South Florida waters have an especially rich and varied array of sea life.

For West Indian plants and animals not closely associated with salt water, the unbridged ocean gap was truly a barrier. Its isolating effect was diminished, however, because the usual movement of air masses and ocean currents is from the West Indies toward Florida. Through most of the year the trade winds blow steadily across the Antilles to South Florida, and in late summer and fall hurricanes sometimes sweep out of the Caribbean along a similar path. That river in the sea we call the Gulf Stream courses along the north coast of Cuba and, a day or two later, the same water may bathe the shores of the Florida Keys. The original individuals of most of the land plants and animals South Florida received from the West Indies made the trip by accident via one of these common carri-

ers. Migrating birds that made a meal of berries in the Bahamas or Cuba and excreted the seeds on the other side of the Gulf Stream must also have played an important role in transporting West Indian plants to South Florida.

The means of transportation available largely determined which terrestrial species of the West Indies were able to reach South Florida. The odds against the success of any crossing were very great, but some forms were better adapted for the journey than others. In general, species that lived near the West Indian coasts were favored. They were more likely to be picked up by winds or swept to sea during storms and also more likely to be landed in

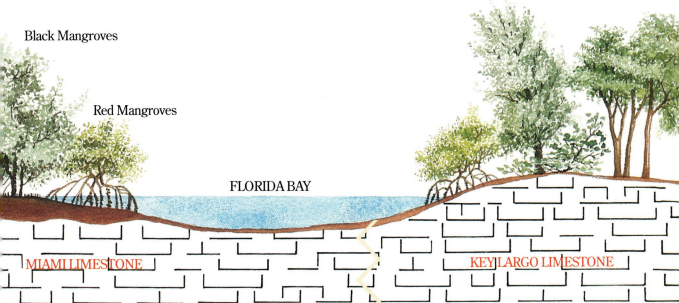

TROPICAL HAMMOCK
ON THE FLORIDA KEYS

Black Mangroves

Red Mangroves

FLORIDA BAY

MIAMI LIMESTONE

KEY LARGO LIMESTONE

ABOVE *This white-crowned pigeon on its nest in a mangrove tree is one of the park's most striking West Indian birds. The white-crowned pigeon feeds on the fruits of many native trees and is one of the major avian seed dispersers.*

INSET *Flotsam on Cape Sable beach after a storm demonstrates one way plants and animals reached Florida.*

closely similar surroundings on the other side. Light weight increased the chances of successful transport. A plant with seeds that could be carried by the wind was more likely to get across than one with heavier seeds. The ability to survive some exposure to salt water was a most desirable quality, whether in the seeds of a plant or the eggs or adults of an animal. And, beyond all such considerations as these, was the mere chance of happening to be in the right place at the right time to be transported to Florida.

Within the last ten thousand years or so, hundreds of land species of the West Indies have made this involuntary passage by wind or water to the Florida shore of the Gulf Stream. The trans-oceanic colonists include a great variety of land plants, many insects and land snails, possibly several kinds of frogs and lizards, and a few land birds. There is ample reason to believe that still more arrivals may be expected. The winds still blow from the southeast, the Gulf Stream still flows north along the Keys, and, in the West Indies, there appear to be many other potential colonizers awaiting only the proper combination of circumstances to move them to South Florida.

The park's animals are a varied assemblage of West Indian and North American forms, offering some animals altogether new to most visitors as well as familiar creatures in a strangely different setting. Most of the animals in both categories are near their range limits, either northern or southern, and species at the fringes of their areas of natural distribution have added interest for the biologist.

Why don't they occur farther north (or farther south)? Does their behavior here differ from that exhibited in the center of the range? A great number of questions of this sort spring to mind, so that a blue jay seen in the pine woods of the park has a dimension of biological significance beyond blue jays elsewhere, because it belongs to the southernmost breeding population of its kind in the eastern United States. As we mention a few of the park's more conspicuous animal inhabitants, it will be of interest to point out from which direction they came to South Florida and to see how they fare in this transition area.

RIGHT *Reduced to about 30 individuals, the Florida panther is making one of its last stands in the eastern United States in the prairies and pinelands of the park's Long Pine Key area.*
INSET *Any park visitor, especially a camper, is likely to meet an inquisitive raccoon.*

THE

CHAPTER THREE

MAMMALS

To return to biogeography for a moment, note that land mammals are seldom able to cross wide sea barriers by natural means. Most of them are too heavy or too little resistant to exposure to be distributed effectively by winds or on drifting debris in ocean currents. For this reason, the West Indies themselves have only a few native mammals and none of the West Indian forms, except one or two rare kinds of bats, has made the crossing to Florida. Virtually all of the land mammals in Florida entered from the north, and most are species well known and widely distributed in the eastern United States. Different species have spread southward into the Florida peninsula for varying distances, but many of them do not range as far as the extreme southern end of the State. As a result, the park has only about 25 kinds of native land mammals, and some of these are uncommon or at least seldom seen. A few others, such as the cottontail rabbit, flying squirrel and spotted skunk, are known in nearby areas and may some day be found in the park.

Those who wish to see land mammals should remember that most are wary and either definitely nocturnal, or much less active during the middle of the day. There is little point in looking for them at high noon and high speed along the main-traveled roads. Instead, walk or drive slowly along back roads and trails in early morning, late evening or at night. In this way, one often can get good views of deer, raccoons, bobcats, otters, and some of the smaller species.

Visitors are usually more interested in the larger mammals and of these species only deer are common in the park. This is the same white-tailed or Virginia deer found throughout the eastern United States. As is true of many wide-ranging, warm-blooded animals, Everglades deer are considerably smaller than deer found farther north. For example, they are about two-thirds the size of deer in Pennsylvania or Wisconsin. This trend reaches its extreme in the miniature key deer of the outer Florida Keys. Protected from hunting for the past 40 years, the deer population in the park has reached a natural balance with its environment.

Deer range throughout the park mainland, occasionally even to islands in northern Florida Bay, but they are scarce on Cape Sable and in the coastal mangrove belt. They are most numerous in the wet prairies around Long Pine Key and the rocky pinelands are also densely webbed with deer trails. Humans, who must traverse the eroded limestone in a ponderous, stumbling walk, can only marvel as deer whisk away on their seemingly fragile legs. In the interior Everglades, the deer are practically amphibious and often wade belly-deep to feed on marsh plants. Extremely high water in the glades, however, forces deer onto the elevated tree islands. There, if flooding is prolonged, they may exhaust the food and many may die of starvation and disease. Such mortality is less frequent in the park than farther north in the Everglades, where water is usually deeper and tree-island refuges fewer. The best places to see deer in the park are the back-country trails on and around Long Pine Key, along the main road from the park entrance to Mahogany Hammock, and along the Shark Valley Road. You need to take extra care if you drive in these areas, particularly at night, because deer often feed along the shoulders or amble across the roads.

To many people, black bears and mountain scenery are the two necessary features of a National Park. Small wonder, then, that Everglades National Park has sometimes been thought rather poorly equipped. To be sure, the park has more black bears than it has mountains, but the few bears in the area have shown little disposition to make themselves visible along roadsides or around campgrounds. With continued protection bears may increase, but the park apparently does not provide very suitable habitat for them. The

most common evidence of their presence is a cabbage palm with the tip torn out, which indicates that a bear has dined on the growing bud of the tree. This confection, the tender "cabbage" which gives the tree its name, is a favored salad of bears and frontier humans in Florida. Bears also have a well-known sweet tooth and sometimes raid hives of bees put out to gather wild honey in areas around the park. And, in times past, they reportedly visited the Cape Sable beaches in summer to feast on sea turtle eggs.

As if to compensate for the woeful scarcity of bears, the park (along with Big Cypress National Preserve and nearby swamplands and ranches) harbors the only wild population of panthers that survives in the eastern United States. The panther is the same beast elsewhere known as mountain lion, cougar, painter, catamount, and puma. The cat of many names once ranged almost throughout the New World from the edge of the Arctic tundra to Patagonia but has been wiped out or greatly depleted over large parts of its former range. Biologists estimate that about 30 panthers remain in the wild in southern Florida and 8 to 10 of these inhabit the eastern part of the park and adjacent lands. Major research and management efforts are underway to assure the survival and increase of panthers in Florida.

Panthers measure as much as seven feet from nose to tip of the long tail and adult males may weigh nearly 150 pounds. Their color is tawny to

grayish, reports of melanistic black panthers have never been verified. Perhaps the reports are related to the fact that most panthers are seen fleetingly at night. Deer and in some areas free-ranging hogs are the panther's staple food. When hunting is good, panthers kill about one deer a week. They also take raccoons, opossums, marsh rabbits, and other medium-sized prey as the opportunity occurs, and lone animals can probably maintain themselves on such prey. Females with kittens, however, must obtain food regularly in deer-sized packages in order to rear their young. Except for brief association when they mate, adult panthers lead solitary lives and range widely. Males, in particular, may have activity areas that cover several hundred square miles. Panthers are difficult to observe even where fairly common, but there are recent sightings along the main park road and back roads around Long Pine Key. The visitor lucky enough to glimpse one has had an authentic encounter with the vanishing American wilderness. Panther tracks, at least three inches across and showing no claw marks, are also impressive and can often be seen in muddy spots along trails and roads.

The bobcat, or wildcat, is common throughout the park mainland, except in the wettest areas. Leggy, with its brown, grizzled coat, dan-

It is said to be the basis for the mermaid myth of old, but the fact bears small resemblance to the fancy. The sailor who first saw in a manatee the likeness of a beautiful girl had an extravagant imagination or had been at sea too long, for the animal's appearance and habits are better described by its alternative name, sea cow.

Manatees are immense, more or less cigar-shaped animals. Very large adults may reach lengths of over 15 feet and weigh close to a ton. They inhabit coastal waters and the lower courses of rivers in the American tropics from Florida (rarely farther north) to northern South America. In the park, they are most often seen in the rivers flowing into Whitewater Bay and along the Gulf Coast. Entirely modified for an aquatic existence, manatees lack external hind limbs, have paddle-like forelimbs and

ABOVE *Power boats and polluted water are the main present-day enemies of the manatee.*

swim by powerful up and down strokes of the broad, flat tail. In their feeding habits they are the cattle of the sea. The pastures they graze are beds of grass-like marine plants growing in shallow, quiet bays and lagoons. Manatees in Florida have suffered because their flesh is highly edible, and from the time of the early Indians until recent years they were hunted extensively. Now protected as an endangered species, the population in Florida numbers about 1,500. Because they are susceptible to cold and may be killed by a sharp drop in water temperature, manatees seek warm-water refuges in winter. Many winter where large central Florida springs discharge constant-temperature water and in the warm effluent of power plants. Others migrate south along the coasts, so that numbers in the park are usually highest in winter. The manatee's main modern enemy, however, is the power boat. Almost every large individual wears its history on its back in propeller scars, and collisions with boats are by far the major cause of mortality. Manatees can move rapidly at need, but in cramped waters, such as canals and boat basins, they are often unable to get out of the way.

The other mammalian inhabitant of the park's coastal waters is the bottlenosed dolphin or porpoise. The name dolphin is also applied to a marine game fish commonly caught in

deep water off Miami and the Keys, but the porpoise is a warm-blooded animal related to the whales. While most of the whales and their relatives are seldom seen near shore, the bottlenosed dolphin regularly ranges into bays and shallow water along the coast and sometimes ventures far up the rivers on the Gulf side of the park. It seems to excel in most departments where the manatee is deficient. Manatees appear to be sluggish creatures and they certainly are difficult to observe. The porpoise, by contrast, is likely to be seen by anyone who does much boating in Florida Bay or along the Gulf Coast, and it enjoys the reputation of being one of the most intelligent and playful of mammals. Trained porpoises are the stars of many exhibits of marine life. Even in the wild, porpoises will often swim beside boats for long distances, jumping gracefully in the wake or diving beneath the boat to appear on the other side, apparently all for the fun of it. They feed on fish, and there can be few more animated sights in nature than that of porpoises charging into a school of mullet, against the background of a sun-drenched Florida Bay scene.

BIRDS

CHAPTER FOUR

OF THE EVERGLADES

Southern Florida has long been known for its rich bird life. Beginning with Audubon's visit 150 years ago, a succession of renowned naturalists explored the area and recorded their observations. Few places in the United States can offer greater variety of beautiful, rare and interesting birds. About 350 different species have been identified in the park and new ones are added to the list nearly every year. Southern Florida's location makes it a sort of crossroads of migratory flight. Many birds that winter in the West Indies migrate along the Florida peninsula. Others that winter in Central and South America and normally fly across the Gulf of Mexico may be grounded in the park in large numbers when they encounter westerly storms during their migrations. The migrants, the numerous resident birds, and the stragglers from the West Indies and the far western United States add up to a changing bird show having something of interest to offer every day of the year.

The large water birds claim the greatest share of attention. The majority of America's species of wading

ABOVE *In late winter, large flocks of many species of wading birds congregate to feed where falling water levels have concentrated fish and other aquatic life.*

INSET *The red-shouldered hawk, the park's most common raptor, feeds extensively on frogs and small snakes. Here one surveys its domain from a dwarf cypress.*

27

birds, shorebirds and waterfowl are found in the park at one season or another. Many of them are nesting residents, including some which seldom range farther north and some which have disappeared from other areas where they once occurred. The water birds provide an unfailing source of interest, whether one is intent on learning the various kinds and observing the details of their life arrangements, or desires just to appreciate the beauty of birds in a landscape.

An important goal in the establishment of Everglades National Park was to protect the nesting areas and feeding grounds of herons and ibis. Present populations of these long-legged, long-necked wading birds are sadly reduced from the great concentrations of earlier days, but many are still present in numbers.

With a few pointers all of the birds are easily recognized. Several dozen well-illustrated bird guides are now available for those who wish to pursue the subject. Some characteristics to notice are general size and color, the shape and color of the beak, and the color of the legs and feet. Also, the bird's method of feeding, its flight, and the kind of habitat it frequents may provide clues to its identity. The herons have straight sharp beaks, fold their necks back when they fly, and feed either by stalking slowly along the water's edge or in the shallows, or by taking

a statuesque pose and waiting for the fish to come to them. The ibis and related forms have beaks either long and down-curved or peculiarly shaped. They fly with their necks fully extended and are more active when feeding than most herons.

The roseate spoonbill is surely the least mistakable of the park's common wading birds. Adults in full breeding dress are garish to say the least–bright pink with carmine epaulets and stickpin, saffron tail, red legs, a black ear patch, bare greenish head, and the spoon-shaped bill that gives them their name. Young birds also have a spoon, but their plumage is white with just a touch of pink and it takes them three years or more to acquire full adult finery. Spoonbills nest on a number of the mangrove keys in Florida Bay from November to March and at times also in the large mixed-species colonies on the southern mainland. In the off-season, adults are most common on Cape Sable and along the Gulf Coast of the park, but the young birds migrate northward as far as southern Georgia. They sometimes appear in numbers in interior fresh water areas of the park where adults are seldom seen. In feeding, the spoonbill swings its odd beak from side to side capturing small minnows, shrimp and aquatic insects from the shallow water. Spoonbills were nearly extinct as nesting birds in Florida around 1940, reduced to a few breeding pairs on one island in Florida Bay. From that low point, they increased to more than 1000 nesting pairs in Florida Bay

in the late 1970s and established new colonies on both coasts of central Florida. More recently, spoonbills in the park have declined to about half their peak nesting numbers. The reasons for the recent decline are not well understood, but it may be related to changes in the upland drainage into Florida Bay.

Two other wading birds, the great white heron and the reddish egret, are closely associated with spoonbills in Florida Bay and they also seldom range inland in the park. The great white is a very large, all-white heron with yellow legs and beak; it is also something of a taxonomic enigma. Great white herons and great blue herons are obviously close relatives. The great blue heron, a familiar species over much of the United States, is common as a winter visitor from the north, and nests in the park on keys in Florida Bay and in tree islands of the Everglades. Great whites are found in coastal areas of the Florida Keys, Cuba, Yucatan, and Venezuela, and, at least in some of these places, they interbreed with great blues. After a lot of waffling on the subject, dominant opinion now holds that the great white is a white color phase of the great blue limited to maritime habitats around the Gulf-Caribbean. However, most mated pairs in Florida Bay are the same color and crossing is fairly uncommon. Whatever its

taxonomic status, the great white has had a checkered history in South Florida. At a time when it was already stressed by human predation on nestlings, the killer hurricane of 1935 reduced the population to about 150. Under protection, numbers rebounded to around 1000 in Florida Bay by the late 1950s, then, quickly regained that number after hurricane Donna in 1960 killed at least one-third of the adults. Great whites now nest on nearly all the keys in Florida Bay that do not have resident raccoons, but recent study suggests that all may not be well. Biologists have found that many great whites get most of their food by panhandling for fish around docks along the Florida Keys and that these birds nest much more successfully than those which still fish in the old way. Such findings raise concern that fish populations in Florida Bay may no longer be adequate to support the large numbers of fish-eating birds that nest there.

In contrast to most of the other wading birds, the reddish egret seems never to have recovered from the slaughter and disturbance of the plume-hunting days early in this century. Probably no more than 300 survive in Florida, and most of these are in the Florida Bay section of the park. The term, reddish, does not accurately describe the bird's color, which is blue-gray on the wings and back and maroon or reddish-brown on the head and neck. A white plumage phase also occurs, but dark individuals are much more common. The two-tone bill, black at the tip and flesh-colored at the base, is a good recognition character and the energetic fishing maneuvers are also distinctive. Instead of quietly stalking its fish, as other herons usually do, the reddish egret lurches and stumbles and dashes about the shallows and mud flats behaving as if it were quite drunk.

Four other kinds of herons are conspicuous in the park scene and all occur commonly in both fresh and salt water areas. The great egret (a.k.a., common egret and American egret) is the large, all-white heron most frequently seen in the park. It is considerably smaller than the great white heron or the great blue, and has a yellow beak and black legs and feet. The snowy egret is also white, but it is smaller still and may be known by its black bill and black legs, with bright yellow feet that have won it the name, "golden slippers." These two egrets were hunted almost to extinction in the early 1900s because of the valuable plumes they develop during the breeding season. Today, they are once more common and nest in several rookeries in the park.

Two others, both about the same size as the snowy egret, are the tricolored and little blue herons. The tricolored heron, a graceful bird called by Audubon "lady of the waters," can always be recognized by its bluish back and white underparts.

The adult little blue heron is dark blue all over, as its name allows, but the immature birds are white, looking much like snowy egrets without the golden slippers. Little blue herons molting from immature to adult plumage wear a patchwork plumage of blue and white blotches. Besides those mentioned, the roll call of park herons includes the green-backed heron, two species of bitterns and two of night herons. They are rather secretive birds of the swamps, but all can be seen along Anhinga Trail.

The wood stork (formerly wood ibis) is the only representative of the stork family that nests in the United States. A mainly white bird, as big as the bigger herons, the wood stork has black-bordered wings, a bare grayish head, heavy curved beak, and dark legs with shocking pink feet. Wood storks escaped the plumehunters largely unscathed, because their feathers had little value and their main nesting colonies were in the remote interior rather than at more accessible places near the coast. In more recent times, their numbers declined slowly, because nesting often failed in drought years, but, as recently as the early 1970s, several thousand pairs nested each winter at Cuthbert Lake and East River rookeries. The past 15 years, however, have brought the wood stork near extinction as a nesting bird in the park. In 1988, a mere 200 pairs tried to nest at Cuthbert Lake late in the season, and, as usual of late years, they failed to rear young.

The resounding crash of the wood stork population has to do with the bird's life history in relation to recent habitat changes in the Everglades. Mainly because the young develop slowly, it takes a pair of wood storks five months to nest and rear a brood–about twice the time needed by large herons. Also, because wood storks feed by touch rather than by sighting their prey, they are most successful in drying marshes and ponds where fish are tightly concentrated. They are unable to feed effectively when water is high and flooding extensive. For this reason, most wood storks leave southern Florida in summer. In the past, the storks used a seasonal succession of drying wetlands throughout the southern Everglades. Now, large areas of higher wetlands outside the park have been drained and developed, and water management in remaining natural marshes, including the park, has often held water levels high well into the dry season, so that only brief and limited drying occurs. In this situation, wood storks often must delay the start of their nesting until March which leaves them too little time to bring off a brood before the next rainy season raises water levels again and disperses fish. At this point it is still uncertain whether water can be managed to produce drying patterns that give wood storks some chance of nesting successfully in the park.

ABOVE *Great blue herons are able to fish in deeper ponds and catch larger prey than most other wading birds. Here one subdues a bass at Anhinga Trail.*

INSET *A mockingbird perched in a paurotis palm illustrates the park's mixture of temperate and tropical life.*

ABOUT *The purple gallinule's long toes support it on spatterdock leaves as it searches for insects.*

Two species of ibis, the white and the glossy, both have long, slender, downcurved beaks and feed mainly on crayfish, crabs and other invertebrates by probing in mud or shallow water. Adult white ibis have black-tipped wings and reddish legs and beak; immature birds are brownish or brownish mottled with white. Glossy ibis look black, except at close range where the bronzy and greenish iridescence of the feathers is evident. Although not as plentiful as it once was, the white ibis is still the most common wading bird in the park and nests in many colonies both in the interior and on islands in Florida Bay. Glossy ibis are uncommon and only occasionally nest in the park.

Two other brownish, long-legged marsh dwellers, not closely related to wading birds but somewhat like them in appearance, are the sandhill crane and the limpkin. Cranes are more common on the drier prairies of central Florida, but a few pairs nest in the Everglades. The limpkin is remarkable both for its diet, chiefly one kind of large marsh snail, and its voice, a night-rending wail which has earned it the name, crying bird.

By this time readers may be asking, "What about the flamingos?" The roll has been called without mentioning the wading bird that most intrigues visitors. Flamingos show up fairly frequently along the south coast of the park, most often on the endless mud flats east of the old town of Flamingo and at times in flocks of up to fifty. Probably most of these birds have escaped from captive flocks in the Miami area, such as the one at Hialeah Race Track, but, of course, one can't be sure they are not wild flamingos from the West Indies. There is no solid evidence that flamingos ever nested in Florida, but, until about 1910, flocks of up to several thousand migrated from the Bahamas into Florida Bay to molt. Flamingos are distant relatives of waterfowl, and, like many ducks and geese, they shed all of their wing feathers at one time and are flightless for a period. No doubt the broad mud flats of Florida Bay gave them some security while flightless. After the closest nesting colonies in the Bahamas were destroyed, however, wild flamingos never again appeared in Florida Bay in large numbers.

Equal in interest to the herons and ibis are the pelicans and related birds, of which five species are found commonly in the park. The five are so unlike in appearance and behavior that one might never guess they were relatives. All eat fish, but each approaches the job of catching them in a different way.

The anhinga, for which Anhinga Trail was named, proceeds like a spear fisherman. It submerges, swims underwater stalking its prey,

and with a quick thrust neatly impales the fish on its straight, sharp-pointed bill. Because of its odd appearance and actions, the anhinga has become a bird of many names. It is sometimes called water turkey, a name perhaps suggested by its glossy black plumage and the buff-colored tips of the tail feathers. Another common name is snake-bird. This seems more appropriate, because the anhinga often swims with its body entirely submerged and with the small head and long, very slender neck protruding above the surface, so that it looks much like a swimming water snake.

The cormorant somewhat resembles the anhinga in appearance and, like it, is accomplished at swimming and diving, but the cormorant's approach to fishing is a more vigorous one. It is a more compactly built bird than the anhinga, with a shorter neck and a strongly hooked beak, and it gets its fish by pursuing and capturing them underwater. Cormorants and anhingas sometimes fish the same waters and at times even nest in the same colonies, but, in general, they divide the underwater fishing areas. The anhinga is chiefly an inhabitant of the fresh water ponds and sloughs, while the cormorant is most common in salt water areas.

The familiar brown pelican, also a coastal bird which rarely ventures inland, nests on many of the

mangrove keys in Florida Bay and along the Gulf Coast, often consorting with cormorants in large colonies. A brown pelican or two, seated on convenient pilings, is an essential ingredient of any shore scene in Florida. When they are not disturbed, brown pelicans become tame and soon learn that an easy living can be had around docks where fishing boats come in. If no handouts are forthcoming, however, the brown pelican has a most effective way of fishing for itself. Its method is to fly over the shallows until a suitable target is sighted and then execute a spectacular power dive crashing the water and trapping fish in its commodious pouch.

Many birds of the western United States seem to drift off course in their fall migrations and wind up wintering in southern Florida, but the white pelican is one that makes this trip regularly and in numbers. White pelicans nest mainly in the northern Great Plains and the mountain states (one well-known colony is located in a lake in Yellowstone National Park), but each winter up to 5,000 birds sojourn in the Everglades from October or November to April. Occasionally a few pass up the return flight and remain in Florida all summer without nesting. Like the brown pelican, the white pelican has a throat pouch which makes a handy creel. Instead of dive-bombing the fish, however, white pelicans usually operate as dip netters, while swimming or wading in shallow water. Sometimes a number of them join in what seems to be a cooperative effort by blocking off a small creek or bay and moving toward shore shoulder to shoulder, each one scooping industriously.

The last, but assuredly not the least, of the group is the frigatebird, also called the man-o-war bird, and, like the white pelican, merely a visitor to the park area. Whereas the pelican is a winter visitor from the far northwest, the frigatebird is mainly a summer visitor coming north to Florida from its nesting places on various Caribbean islets. Frigatebirds are so short-legged that they are nearly helpless on the ground. Once aloft, the deeply forked tail and long, narrow wings cease to be encumbrances and give them unmatched mastery of the air. They can hang motionless in the teeth of a gale, attain bursts of speed without noticeable effort, and perform turns and vertical dives from great height. All of this aerial agility is put to use in their fishing. Frigatebirds often catch their own dinners by interrupting the flight of a flying fish or picking up other fish swimming near the surface. They also obtain food by acts of piracy, harassing a gull or pelican until the hapless victim disgorges its catch, and then deftly seizing the ill-gotten fish in midair.

The birds of this group seem to specialize in donning odd adornments for the breeding season. The area of bare skin around the eye of the male anhinga becomes bright blue as the mating season approaches. White pelicans develop a peculiar horn-like growth atop the huge beak. However, male frigatebirds easily take the prize for nuptial ornamentation. During courtship they inflate and display an air sac on the throat until it looks like a livid scarlet balloon. Frigatebirds have been found nesting west of Key West at Marquesas Keys and Dry Tortugas, but are not yet known to nest in the park. However, males with inflated throat pouches are sometimes seen at keys in the park where frigatebirds roost in large numbers in summer.

In addition to the more conspicuous forms already mentioned, the marshes and lakes of the park harbor large concentrations of ducks and coots. Sandpipers, plovers and related shorebirds crowd the tidal mud flats, and many kinds of terns and gulls fish the coastal waters. The majority of these smaller water birds are winter visitors, but a few especially striking ones, such as the purple gallinule, are year-round residents.

Visitors to the area should remember that the present bird life of Everglades National Park is only a remnant and a memory of what was one of the great wildlife spectacles of the North American continent. In its original condition, peninsular Florida was a veritable wonderland of birds. Its shores and coastal lagoons and the interior expanses of marshland, lake and swamp offered virtually limitless accommodation for water birds of every description. The first naturalists who sailed up the St. Johns River and along the southern coasts describe scenes the like of which no one will see in Florida again, the undisturbed abundance of water birds in a land ideally suited to maintain them. In 1774 on the lower St. Johns, William Bartram recorded that sleep was almost impossible, because of "the continual noise and restlessness of the sea fowl...all promiscuously lodging together, and in such incredible numbers that the trees were entirely covered." Of Sandy Key in the park in 1832, Audubon wrote, "The flocks of birds that covered the shelly beaches and those hovering overhead, so astonished us that we could for awhile scarcely believe our eyes." In all of America's rich display of native wildlife, there were few scenes that bear close comparison to the spectacular bird concentrations of primeval Florida.

Much water has flowed down the Everglades since the days of Bartram and Audubon, and much that should have come down has flowed elsewhere. The extravagant abundance of birds chronicled by these early naturalists could not fail to decline, if humans were to occupy Florida and turn the land to domestic uses. Man, in the role both of guardian and despoiler, has long been the dominant factor in the lives of the large wading birds that are the most interesting and conspicuous part of Florida's avian scene.

Most of the water birds found in the park are also found in the West Indies, but, with the notable exception of the flamingo, they are more common today on the Florida side of the Gulf Stream. Of West Indian land birds, only a few species nest in southern Florida, although a number of others occur as rare stragglers. In Florida, the West Indian land birds reside chiefly near the coast where they find mangrove swamps and tropical hardwood forests nearly identical with some habitats they occupy in Cuba and the Bahamas.

Most interesting of the lot is the white-crowned pigeon, a large, dark blue pigeon with a white cap. It nests on the keys in Florida Bay and feeds on the fruit of pigeon plum, wild fig, poisonwood, and other hammock trees. A few white-crowns winter in the park, but most of them migrate back to the West Indies in fall. Other West Indian forms are the mangrove cuckoo, gray kingbird and black-whiskered vireo. The latter two are common and conspicuous summer residents, but the mangrove cuckoo is a secretive bird, probably not rare yet seldom seen. Several West Indian land birds seem to be extending their nesting areas in Flor-

ida, and others, such as the Cuban golden warbler and West Indian cave swallow, are known to have colonized Florida in recent decades.

Aside from the small West Indian contingent, the common land birds of the park are wide-ranging forms and will be old friends to any well-versed bird watcher from farther north. A large proportion of the land birds of eastern North America are found in the park, either as winter residents or passing migrants, with various western species, such as the scissor-tailed flycatcher, thrown in for good measure. In contrast to the great variety of winter visitors and migrants, however, rather few land birds remain to nest in the area.

The nesting land birds are again mainly well-known ones; cardinals and towhees in the thickets, blue jays and bob-white in the pinelands, meadowlarks in the open glades, and yellowthroats and red-winged blackbirds in the sloughs. In the park, most of them reach the far southern edge of their ranges in the eastern United States. Included in the list, however, are the few species rarer or less widely familiar. Wild turkeys are occasionally seen in the Long Pine Key section, especially around live oak hammocks where they can find acorns for food. The pileated woodpecker, a striking, crested species as big as a crow, is common in most of the forested areas, and often digs its squarish nest holes in the trunks of

cabbage palms. About 50 pairs of bald eagles nest in the park, on keys in Florida Bay, and along the Gulf coast. The bald eagle population is stable and productive, but the same may not be true of the park's 150-odd nesting pairs of ospreys. As with many fish-eating birds of park estuaries, osprey numbers seem to be declining in recent years.

To close an account of the birds of the park, no better subject could be chosen than the swallow-tailed kite. This handsome black and white hawk, possessing a swallow's speed and grace, serves well to sum up the story-book quality of Florida bird life. These kites once ranged widely in the South and the Mississippi Valley, but they offer too tempting a target to survive long in settled regions.

In the park they are still fairly common, arriving in late February or March and migrating south again in September. The kites are among the least earthbound of birds. They catch their food in flight and often eat on the wing as well. Their prey includes large insects, such as dragon flies, lizards and small snakes lifted deftly out of tree tops, and young birds plucked from the nest. In midsummer, after their nesting is completed, swallow-tailed kites often assemble in pre-migratory gatherings of as many as several hundred birds. The effortless acrobatics displayed on such occasions are one of the great sights of the bird world.

THE

CHAPTER FIVE

REPTILES AND AMPHIBIANS

Except for the crocodile and perhaps a few kinds of small frogs and lizards from the West Indies, the reptiles and amphibians reached the region by coming south from the continental mainland. Many failed to penetrate as far as South Florida, which has fewer species of these groups than do many other places in the southeastern United States. The known fauna of the park includes three or four kinds of salamanders, six of lizards, ten land and fresh water turtles and several kinds of sea turtles, 12 species of frogs and toads, and 23 species of snakes. Many of these animals are rare or of such retiring habits that they are unlikely to be seen unless one makes a special search for them. A few, however, are more visible or audible elements in the Everglades, or have particular interest for other reasons.

The salamanders may be passed over quickly. All are aquatic and usually live under dense vegetation in and around ponds and canals. The frogs are less likely to be overlooked, if only because of the deafening commotion raised by the males during rainy periods, especially in summer. Two kinds of green tree frogs are often seen resting on vegetation in shady humid spots, or catching insects around lights at night. The big southern bull frog, or pig frog, provides many of the frogleg dinners on restaurant menus, and also the grunting bass notes from the marsh at Anhinga Trail. Other species are little in evidence during the dry season, but when summer rains begin the nightly clamor of their breeding choruses dominates the land. Sometimes half a dozen different kinds of frogs and toads, some with voices far out of proportion to their size, blend their efforts from a single rain pool to attain a truly memorable din.

The anole, or Florida chameleon, is a small arboreal lizard commonly seen in many parts of the park. Like the true chameleons of the Old World it is able to vary its body color, with a range from grass green to brown or grayish. Sometimes the change results in a hue which more nearly matches the color of its background, but this is not always the case. Many other factors, including air temperature, help determine what

INSET *Native green anoles, seen here, have been crowded out in some areas by introduced Cuban anoles.*

ABOVE *Most of the park's American crocodiles are found in northeastern Florida Bay and around Flamingo.*

color is assumed in a given situation. Male anoles fight viciously during the breeding season, for all the world like tiny dragons, and they are provided with a flap of loose skin on their throats which is elevated to form a bright red fan during courtship activities or in threat displays to other males.

Several varieties of West Indian lizards have been accidentally established around Key West and Miami, but the reef gecko, a tiny brownish species found in the hammocks of the park, is a West Indian form which probably reached South Florida without human assistance. Some of the introduced West Indian forms, such as the Cuban tree frog and Cuban anole, have spread widely in southern Florida crowding out the native species.

Of the turtles in the park, the box turtle is probably the one most often observed. It is a terrestrial species commonly seen crossing roads. The soft-shelled turtle and two kinds of fresh water terrapins are common in the deeper Everglades sloughs, such as Anhinga Trail, and are often preyed upon by alligators. In spring and early summer, these three turtles, and also the snapping turtle, sometimes deposit their eggs in holes they dig in the sides of road embankments built across the marsh.

Along the coast and around the mangrove keys in Florida Bay is found the diamondback terrapin, a member of the same breed which enjoys such high culinary renown in the Chesapeake Bay region. They sometimes can be seen in abundance at high tide on the banks of the canals and streams along the south coast.

By all odds the most interesting of the park's turtles are the true sea turtles, large, entirely aquatic, mostly tropical forms which inhabit the open ocean and rarely come to shore, except to lay their eggs. In earlier times, four different kinds of sea turtles nested on the Florida beaches, but excessive hunting of the eggs and adults and real estate development of beach areas have greatly reduced their numbers. Today only one species, the loggerhead turtle, nests at all commonly in the park. Another large sea turtle, the hawksbill, or tortoiseshell, is often seen around coral reefs on the ocean side of Key Largo.

Favored nesting areas in the park are the long beaches fronting on the Gulf of Mexico at Cape Sable and Highland Point. Here female loggerhead turtles haul themselves ashore at night in spring and early summer, particularly during the period of highest full-moon tides. The eggs, usually 100 or more and looking something like large ping-pong balls, are laid in excavations in the sand above high tide. The females are extremely vulnerable during the several hours re-

quired to dig the nest hole, deposit the eggs and cover them, and not long ago it was a common practice of fishermen at Cape Sable and elsewhere to gather the turtle eggs, and to turn nesting females on their backs and butcher them on the beach.

Many predators other than man are aware of this treasure trove of food to be found in the sands. Raccoons, and occasionally bears, patrol the beaches prospecting for turtle eggs. In nests surviving these combined onslaughts the eggs hatch within about two months. Full-grown adults may weigh 300 pounds or more, with shells as much as three feet in length. The hatchlings, tiny facsimiles no more than two inches long, immediately take to the water, and, with luck in a sea beset with dangers for so small an animal, they may some day return to continue the cycle.

The Everglades is often portrayed with some justice as the happy hunting ground for all sorts of creatures that crawl and hop. At rare intervals when water is extremely high in the glades, the number of snakes in view along the roads may seem to justify one's wildest notions of reptilian abundance, but these represent animals from a wide surrounding area concentrated on a few spots of high ground left available. Under usual conditions, the ordinary visitor will not find the country unduly overrun with snakes and their kin.

Although the park harbors a goodly variety of snakes, including some beautifully marked and interesting harmless species, as well as several equally interesting but venomous ones, many visitors express relief that their uneasy expectations of finding snakes in great numbers turn out to be unfounded. In part, this is because snakes are less active during the dry winter months; in part it is due to the fact that popular notions of the abundance of serpents in the Everglades are somewhat exaggerated.

Most interest in snakes centers on the poisonous species of which four are found in the area. The commonest is probably the pygmy rattler, a miniature rattlesnake seldom over two feet long. At the other extreme is the diamondback rattlesnake which often attains a length of six feet and is without question one of the world's most dangerous snakes. The water moccasin, or cottonmouth, is found around sloughs and canals. The coral snake occurs rarely, most often in hammock areas of the park.

Both of the latter species have "look-alikes"–several harmless snakes that are somewhat similar to the venomous ones in appearance. Three kinds of large brownish water snakes also inhabit the ponds and sloughs and are often confused with water moccasins, while both the scarlet snake and the scarlet king snake are marked with bright red, black and yellow rings resembling the pattern of the coral snake.

It is well to remember that there are poisonous snakes in the park and to be careful when walking at night or in dense vegetation, but the danger is not great. By now, Everglades National Park has hosted millions of visitors but has had only four or five instances of snake bite, none of which was serious.

The handsome, glossy blue-black indigo snake is found throughout the park and is one of the most interesting of the harmless species. It sometimes reaches the imposing length of eight feet, but is altogether mild-mannered and docile in behavior. Other interesting forms are the red rat snake and the yellow rat snake, both primarily rodent eaters and often found around buildings. The Florida king snake has a blotched or speckled pattern of black and light yellow and, in addition to rodents, feeds on other snakes, including the poisonous ones. Among the smaller species, two of those most frequently seen are the ribbon snake and the rough green snake.

The alligator is Florida's leading reptilian citizen, and the animal visitors are most interested in seeing. The many alligator farms and exhibits scattered along the length of the state testify to the strength of this interest. Everglades National Park, however, is one of the few places where wild alligators can be observed readily and in numbers. They have top billing in the park's wildlife show, and sometimes behave as if they knew it.

Alligators occur throughout the interior of the park, and, in summer when heavy run-off of water from the glades freshens the brackish streams and bays, they move into the coastal sections of Florida Bay and the Gulf of Mexico. During times of high water they may appear almost anywhere, even in shallow ditches beside the roads. As the glades gradually go dry in winter and spring, the gators begin to seek the deeper ponds and sloughs, and, in drought years, the concentrations of large saurians basking around pools and canals may seem like the reenactment of some scene from the earth's dim past.

RIGHT *The strikingly patterned green tree frog is one of the most widespread amphibians of the park.*

The seasonal cycle of rising and falling water is the dominant fact in the lives of all the animals of the Everglades. In this ecological drama the alligator often plays the role of a natural hydraulic engineer, much as the beaver does on mountain streams. Big alligators frequently dig ponds at low places in the glades and return to these private retreats each dry season, deepening and enlarging the pond as the years pass. Such ponds, called "gator holes," provide places where marsh snails, frogs, and fish can survive the dry months to repopulate the glades when summer rains come and the water rises again. Until a few years ago, alligators were hunted so persistently for their hides that they had disappeared from parts of southern Florida and were much reduced in numbers everywhere. With the protection afforded by the park, they are now increasing, and their increase should result in more secure dry-season living accommodations for many other animals of the glades.

If one watched a spot like the ponds at Anhinga Trail carefully enough, he could soon become acquainted with the alligator's whole life history. The chief food items of the adults seem to be fish and turtles, but any bird or mammal straying close to a hungry alligator risks being added to the bill of fare. Mating occurs in April and May, and, as the breeding season approaches, the bellowing of

the adult bulls adds a new note to the cacophony of the swamp. At this time, the bulls become more and more intolerant, and smaller individuals incautious enough to trespass are likely to be disposed of in short order.

The female alligator builds a nest consisting of a mound of mud and rotting vegetation, lays her eggs in a cavity in the heap of rubbish she has scraped together, and guards the spot until the eggs hatch, usually in late summer or early fall.

Alligator hatchlings average about 10 inches long. They grow at the rate of a foot a year for the first few years and then more slowly, and become adult in about 10 years. Alligators are long-lived, continue to grow throughout their lives, and may reach very large size. There is said to be one reliable record of a 19-footer, but individuals 12 or 13 feet in length are about the largest that have been seen in the park. Authentic records of unprovoked attacks by wild alligators on human beings are rare, at least in modern times, but any big alligator should be treated with caution. The half-tame alligators that live in the lakes and canals of settled areas often are accustomed to being fed by humans and are much more dangerous and unpredictable than wild animals.

A question sometimes asked by park visitors meeting alligators

face to face for the first time is, "Are alligators and crocodiles different, or just two names for the same thing?" The answer is: they are related species, animals cut to much the same pattern with numerous similarities of behavior and physical structure, but differing in many details. If the visitor should then ask, "Are there any crocodiles in the park?" The answer, happily, is yes.

Whereas the alligator is widely distributed in the Atlantic coastal plain from South Carolina to Texas, the crocodile is found in the United States only in a limited section of southern Florida. It is another species which probably reached Florida from the West Indies and one for which Everglades National Park provides an essential sanctuary. At one time crocodiles occurred as far north as the Palm Beach area in Florida, but their numbers have diminished, because of hunting and the settlement of the country, until today they are seldom seen outside of Florida Bay and a few places in the Florida Keys and along the southern Gulf Coast.

Less is known about the crocodile's life and habits than those of its more common relative. Crocs seem to be shyer and are much more difficult to observe. In Florida, they are seldom found far from salt water, and

the nests they build on the narrow beaches of Florida Bay are great heaps of sand and shell. Crocodiles and alligators may at times be found in the same area, but in general each keeps to its own domain, the gators inland in fresh water and the crocs along the coast and offshore. Crocodiles can best be recognized in the field by their color (olive-gray or greenish where alligators, except very young ones, are blackish) and by the narrow tapering snout in contrast to the broad shovel-shaped snout of the alligator.

Everglades National Park has nearly as many kinds of fishes, around 300, as it has of birds and the park is as renowned among fishermen as among bird watchers. Together the two groups of enthusiasts make up a large proportion of the park's specifically oriented visitors. The fishermen are attracted by a number of well-known game and/or food fishes including largemouth bass in the interior ponds and sloughs and tarpon, bonefish, snook, red drum, sea trout, barracuda, and several kinds of snappers and groupers in Florida Bay and along the Gulf Coast. And, more important than the excitement they provide for anglers, fishes also are the principal food of many other animals of the Everglades.

The fishes of the park's salt and brackish waters tend to be widely distributed in similar habitats of the West Indies and beyond. The freshwater fishes are biogeographically more diverse. A recent review listed 92 species that have been found in the fresh waters of southern Florida. About a quarter of these–including the bowfin, several minnows, a pike, a sucker, the largemouth bass, and a number of other sunfish–found their way into the Everglades from the north. This group is small, because past pathways for migration have not allowed freshwater fishes easy access to the southern part of the Florida peninsula. About two-thirds of the fishes in fresh water were originally

salt water forms and these tend to be of more tropical affinities. Some species are now limited to freshwater habitats, some move freely between fresh and salt water and others are casual visitors from coastal waters. Finally, a sizable and increasing segment of the fish fauna of the freshwater Everglades is made up of escaped, non-native fishes originally imported into South Florida for the aquarium trade from tropical areas around the world. A number of these species are becoming widely distributed in the park and they may be competing with the native freshwater fishes.

The importance of fish populations in Everglades food webs of both fresh and salt water areas can scarcely be overstated. Virtually all of the park's water birds and raptors such as the osprey and bald eagle eat mainly fish. In freshwater areas, breeding by wading birds is closely tied to the availability of fish as prey through the annual cycle of flooding and drying of the Everglades. The recent drastic decline of wading birds in southern Florida is closely related to the failure of this once-predictable cycle, largely because water has remained high and fishes unavailable during the usual season of drying.

THE

CHAPTER SIX

FISHES AND INVERTEBRATES

Any brief review of the invertebrates of the region (the animals without backbones) must necessarily be limited to a few of the most conspicuous kinds. Even a bare list of the varied forms of life represented would occupy far more pages than are in this book. The really important invertebrate animals are the tiny and extremely abundant forms that stand near the base of the food pyramid in both fresh and salt water habitats. These creatures eat minute plant life and provide food for small fishes and other aquatic animals, which in turn feed larger fishes, which are eaten by egrets, otters, etc., but the beginning links of the chain are visible only with a microscope. Several larger invertebrates of freshwater areas are directly linked to upper levels of food chains. Thus, crayfish and freshwater prawns are a substantial part of the diet of the white ibis and little blue heron, and the apple snail is practically the sole food of snail kites and limpkins.

The variety of marine invertebrate life in the park is limited by the narrow range of available habitat conditions. Only forms characteristic of shallow water and mud or shell bot-

LEFT *The handsome zebra butterfly is a South Florida representative of a group that is varied and widespread in the New World tropics.*
FAR LEFT *A golden orb weaver spider at home.*

mouths of the Gulf Coast rivers, and because of them a boat passage from the Gulf into such streams as Lostmans River or Rodgers River requires delicate navigation.

Of the crustaceans, blue crabs and stone crabs are fairly common, and a few of the big Florida lobster or crawfish can be found in Florida Bay. Fiddler crabs are present in seething abundance in all the muddy tidal areas and are fed upon by raccoons and some birds. Heavy runs of shrimp occur at times and Florida Bay and the coastal bays of the park are a major nursery area for young shrimp, which, later in life, are caught on the commercial shrimping grounds around Dry Tortugas.

The invertebrate animals of land habitats in southern Florida include many that are identical with or closely related to West Indian species, but biogeographic patterns vary between groups. Thus, the ants are mainly of northern origin, but the butterflies and land snails are pre-

toms occur commonly, while the more varied life of the coral reefs and rocky shores of South Florida is largely absent. The mollusks and crustaceans are the most evident of the marine invertebrates. The beaches of the park are composed almost entirely of broken fragments of shells heaped up by the waves, and a good variety of sea shells can be

found at some locations. These include several striking ones such as the angel wing and the crown conch.

Oyster bars are frequent along the Gulf as far south as Harney River, and oysters also often attach to mangrove roots. The oyster bars seem to develop particularly well in the

dominantly West Indian. As discussed earlier, the animals that arrived from the West Indies were the ones best adapted to be carried by winds or on debris drifting in ocean currents.

The large tree snails of the type known by the Latin name, Liguus, are perhaps the most beautiful and unusual of the West Indian forms and are certain to claim the attention of park visitors. Outside of southern Florida, Liguus snails occur only on the islands of Cuba and Hispaniola in the West Indies. The Florida shells are most closely related to types found in Cuba, but in Florida they have developed many new color varieties. These tree snails grow to be 2 to 2 1/2 inches long, and have a seemingly endless array of bright patterns. Solid color forms range from white to deep orange to almost black, while others feature variegated patterns involving bands, narrow lines, or mottling of brown, yellow, green, and smoky blue on various background colors. More than 50 different patterns have been distinguished and new ones are still found occasionally.

Because of their beauty and biological interest, tree snails have attracted the attention of collectors for many years. Some of the color forms may have been drastically reduced by too much collecting, but, as is true of most of the retreating natural life of southern Florida, the bulldozer has been a far greater enemy

to Liguus than the most unprincipled of collectors. Tree snails are intimately adapted to life in the tropical hammocks. They are becoming increasingly rare and some varieties have entirely disappeared because of the recent wholesale clearing of hammock vegetation in the Keys and along the southeast coast. The clear prospect for the future is that tree snails will survive in numbers in Florida only on protected land. Some of the forms most threatened by land development have been re-established at safe locations within the park.

In their hammock homes, tree snails are active chiefly at night and in humid, cloudy weather. At such times they feed actively on minute mould-like fungi growing on smooth-barked tropical trees, such as the wild tamarind and Jamaica dogwood. The snails scrape their food from the bark with rasp-like mouth parts. Where the fungal growth is profuse, it often is possible to see tree snail feeding trails, narrow clean-scraped paths winding along the trunks and larger branches of the trees.

During the winter, tree snails perform a sort of hibernation to protect themselves from drying. They may seek hiding places in cavities or under loose bark or attach themselves to trees in the open by secreting a sticky material that hardens to fasten them firmly. Even in winter, however, they often become active during rainy spells and may be seen crawling about over the vegetation.

The beginning of sustained rains in spring initiates breeding activities and a period of rapid growth when the snails resume building their multicolored shells. Liguus is a bisexual organism, each snail possessing both male and female reproductive organs. Cross fertilization is the rule, but a particular individual may assume the roles of both sexes during a breeding season.

Eggs are ready to be laid after about two months and are deposited, usually immediately after a rain, in shallow nests dug in the leaf litter near the base of a food tree. From eight to as many as fifty eggs make up a clutch. The eggs usually remain in the ground during the winter dry season and hatch the following spring; the just-hatched youngsters possess a perfect shell about 1/8 inch in diameter. They grow rapidly in their first summer, adding several complete whorls to the shell and attaining a length of as much as an inch. In succeeding years, growth becomes much slower. The enemies of tree snails, in addition to collectors and bulldozers, include rats, raccoons, opossums, and various birds.

National Parks are so commonly thought of in terms of their value for protection of the larger birds and mammals that it is easy to forget they also provide refuge for a host of smaller creatures. The insect world of southern Florida is a particularly interesting and varied one. It includes many species of bizarre appearance and beautiful coloration, many with involved and remarkable life histories, and many that are still little known. Almost every specialist who works in the area finds that his collections include species new to science, or West Indian forms not found before in the United States. Some day the park area will furnish material for a fascinating book on insects alone.

Doug Perrine

ABOVE *This Liguus tree snail is one of more than 50 named color forms.*
FAR LEFT *A row of thorn bugs on a twig illustrates the bizarre diversity of insect life.*

ABOVE TOP *The archaic spotted gar is a common predatory fish in ponds and sloughs.*
ABOVE CENTER *The tarpon is a favorite game fish of estuarine and ocean waters.*
ABOVE BOTTOM *Garish colors of the lubber grasshopper may be a warning to potential predators.*

45

A great wealth of native plant life was once one of southern Florida's foremost natural glories. Even today, after the destruction wrought by almost a century of lumbering, land clearing, drainage, and man-caused fire, enough remains to make South Florida an area of outstanding botanical interest. One of the key reasons for establishing Everglades National Park was to preserve some of the region's rare and unusual plants in their natural surroundings. Additional small areas of plant communities not found in the park should be set aside in order to save a truly representative sample of the native flora. Without such protection, many interesting plants, particularly those found only in the hammocks and pine-palm woods of the Keys, are likely to be erased from the Florida scene within a few years.

The flora of the park includes about 1000 different kinds of seed-bearing plants and many others representing the more primitive and more simply constructed groups, such as ferns, mosses, and lichens. Although the botany of the park area has been studied for many years, exploration has continued to add new plants to the list. Doubtless many others await discovery. The professional botanist or the visitor who enjoys seeing uncommon and novel plants will find that he can spend weeks in the park without exhausting the floristic diversity of its hammocks, pinelands, and prairies.

The park is particularly well-stocked with woody plants, nearly 120 species of trees, plus many shrubs and vines, and this rich assortment of the unfamiliar is often a source of great bewilderment to the visitor.

The distribution of plants in the area provides our best illustration of the location of zonal boundaries. Within South Florida, plants derived from the West Indian tropics predominate southward and near the coasts, while temperate zone species from continental North America become more prominent northward and at interior localities. In the usual course of events, visitors have their first close contact with the park's native plants on the Gumbo-limbo Trail at Royal Palm or at Flamingo. In these areas the dominance of tropical trees is complete or nearly so, and the initial confusion of the northerner interested in plants is often equally complete.

Fresh from country where one need not be a botanist to distinguish the common trees, the park visitor enters forests where the trees are not only unknown but disconcertingly alike. Especially distressing is the absence of distinctive leaf outlines which give easy clues to a tree's identity. Instead of the familiar leaf forms of oak and maple and elm, most of the leaves appear to have been cut from the same pattern, glossy and hard-textured, more or less elliptical in shape and often with pointed tips.

There is good reason for this general similarity. It represents the sum of various structural adaptations of leaves to restrict water loss in a region where the dry season is sometimes prolonged, and, of course, most of the likenesses are not nearly as exact as they seem. One soon comes to know the satinleaf tree by the bright cinnamon color of the underside of the leaves and the gumbo-limbo by its bronze bark. Other species sort themselves out, because their leaves are compound, or by differences in leaf outline not noticed at first. It is possible to learn to recognize the common West Indian trees of the park in short order, once one is past that bewildering first impression. A less abrupt introduction to the park flora would be possible if one could enter at the northwest and work his way from hammock to hammock across the Everglades and finally to the coast. In hammocks at the beginning of such a route a visitor could find a number of trees with which he might be on speaking terms—several oaks, a species of ash, red maple, hackberry, and others. In and around tree islands in the glades, would be willow, elderberry, cypress,

bay, wax myrtle, holly, and magnolia, familiar at least by name. And, along the way, the confusing tropical species would be met a few at a time instead of en masse.

At Royal Palm some northern trees persist in the forest flora. Hackberry, red mulberry, sumac, and persimmon are examples, yet, except for the live oak, all are uncommon and submerged in the profusion of subtropical growth. By the time the coastal area of Flamingo is reached, the last northern representative has been left behind. Botanically, one has arrived in the West Indies.

One interesting point about some northern trees here at the southern fringe of their ranges is that they retain the characteristic of dropping their leaves in the fall. Some, such as cypress, remain leafless through the winter, while others grow new leaves again after a brief interval. The leaves of sumac and persimmon, two plants which contribute to the brilliant displays of autumn foliage in many northern woods, also turn red before they fall in far southern Florida. A number of the tropical tree species are also deciduous, but in a much more irregular fashion. Many tend to lose leaves gradually during the winter and may stand nearly bare by spring, if the dry season is unusually severe or prolonged. Others—mahogany, Jamaica dogwood, and coral bean, for example—regularly drop their leaves in spring, produce flowers on nearly bare twigs, and put out new leaves almost at once.

Among trees, the palms most clearly symbolize the tropics, and the park is not deficient in this essential. Eight of the 14 kinds of palms native to the United States grow in southern Florida and six of these are found in the park. In addition, the coconut palm is well established at Cape Sable (once the site of a commercial coconut plantation) and elsewhere near beaches, but it probably is not native to the area. Planted date palms also grow around the locations of some former homesteads.

Of the native species, the royal palm is surely the handsomest and is widely planted as an ornamental. In the wild, smooth, grayish, cylindrical trunks may reach a height of more than 100 feet and lift dark green crowns of featherlike leaves high above the associated growth. Royal palms are found in the park only at Royal Palm and several other hammocks in that vicinity and at a few places along the Gulf Coast. It is possible that the present distribution may indicate that the fruit was a food item utilized by the early Indians, because several of the locations where royal palms now grow are ancient Indian mounds.

The cabbage palmetto, is the common large palm tree which occurs throughout the park. Saw palmetto occurs abundantly in all the rocky pineland, usually as a low-growing plant, but occasional individuals with erect stems are found.

LEFT *Gumbo-limbo, with its bronze bark, is one of the most common and most recognizable trees in the tropical hammock.*
INSET BELOW *A thriving strangler fig consolidates its grip on a live oak tree.*

Silver palm grows as an attractive small tree on the Keys, but in the pine woods of the park it is usually a stemless plant easily overlooked among the saw palmettos. It also occurs, or once did, in pineland areas throughout Dade county.

The Florida thatch palm found along the north shore of Florida Bay is more common in the Keys. It has circular leaves not folded like those of the cabbage palm, a slender trunk and white fruits. The similar brittle thatch palm grows on Big Pine Key. The paurotis, or saw-cabbage palm, occurs in hammocks in a narrow belt along the mangrove edge of the southern Everglades, and is easily seen from the road to Flamingo. It forms dense clumps of up to several dozen stems 30 to 40 feet tall. The fronds resemble those of saw pal-metto and the stems of the leaves are also edged with saw-like teeth. Out-side the park, this palm is found in Florida only at a few spots in the Big Cypress and in western Cuba and northern Central America.

Of the many other kinds of native tropical trees it is possible here to note only a few with qualities of special interest.

Three kinds of mangrove trees, red, black, and white, form the man-grove swamps which occupy all low-lying shores in South Florida. Some-times they are arranged in fairly dis-tinct belts, with red mangroves form-ing the coastal edge of the swamp

ABOVE LEFT
Coral bean is one of the park's most striking flowers.
ABOVE CENTER
Star-like spider lilies bloom in the wet prairies and around ponds.
ABOVE RIGHT
Ribbed, bright-green, glossy leaves and red berries identify wild coffee shrubs.
BELOW *The tran-sition zone be-tween mangrove and sawgrass has a sparse growth of shrubby red man-groves.*

and extending into shallow water offshore, while the other two grow farther inland. Elsewhere, as in the superb forests along the lower courses of the Gulf Coast rivers, all three are found together. The three mangroves are not close botanical relatives; each belongs to a different family of plants. They are associated because of a common ability to grow in areas subject to overflow by sea water and in highly saline soil. The mangroves do not require salt but they can tolerate it to escape competi-tion. All the mangroves have been grown experimentally in fresh water, and red mangrove is common along the southern edge of the Everglades in areas sea water seldom reaches except during severe hurricanes.

The red mangrove is notable for its stilt roots and pendent cigar-shaped seedlings which begin grow-ing before they drop from the parent tree. The seedlings may float long distances in ocean currents and take root wherever they are stranded in shallow water. This highly efficient means of oceanic dispersal explains why the red mangrove and closely related species occur on tropical shores the world around.

Black mangrove may be recognized by the numerous, quill-like pneumatophores, or breathing tubes, projecting upward from the shallow roots. The leaves are whitish on the underside where they are often coated with salt. This species is also one of the area's commercial honey plants, particularly along the Keys where one often sees beehives set out in the swamps when black mangroves are in flower.

White mangrove is widespread in the park, but it is less common than the other two forms and does not possess such striking structural peculiarities. The largest trees measured in the big Shark River mangrove forest were white mangroves. Another tree which is sometimes associated with the mangroves and also forms extensive pure-stand forests on its own, is buttonwood. It is notable as the source of most of the picturesque "driftwood" of South Florida commerce. These ornamental pieces are the weathered, contorted trunks and branches of storm-killed buttonwood trees, and may or may not have drifted.

Three plants found in the park have sap toxic to humans. Contact with them can cause dermatitis which may be severe in particularly sensitive individuals. One of these is the widely distributed, white-fruited vine, poison ivy. The other two, both West Indian trees which reach their northern range limits in southern Florida, are poisonwood and manchineel. Poisonwood belongs to the same family as poison ivy, but its compound leaf usually has five leaflets instead of three and the fruits are orange oval berries in dangling clusters. Poisonwood is a common tree in most of the hammocks and pine woods, where it may be dwarfed by fire. Its clear, sticky sap turns black on exposure.

The name manchineel comes from the Spanish word, manzanillo, meaning little apple. The leaves and growth form are at least vaguely reminiscent of an apple tree, and the fruit could be mistaken for a green crab apple except for its large, woody core and very thin layer of white flesh. Manchineel trees occur only near the coast and, although some may be seen along the Bear Lake trail and near Coot Bay, they are most abundant farther east in areas park visitors seldom reach. Many highly imaginative tales are told of the "deadly" machineel, but, in fact, its effects differ little from those of better-known, related poisonous plants. Contact with the milky sap causes blistering of the skin and oral inflammation.

Among the native tropical trees of southern Florida are many which produce heavy, hard wood valued for fine cabinetwork and other uses. Some examples are crabwood, leadwood, fiddlewood and lignum-vitae. In most cases, perhaps fortunately, the large trees were too few and scattered to make commercial exploitation practicable. An exception is the mahogany, of which sizable specimens were common on some of the Florida Keys and along the south coast. Sailors who came to cut mahogany for ship timbers were among the early European visitors to South Florida shores, and small lumbering enterprises were occasionally renewed in the area until recent years. Mahogany is still a common tree in the park, but large specimens are rare today except in a few hammocks along the isolated southern edge of the Everglades. One of these, named Mahogany Hammock, is accessible by road, and there visitors may see living mahogany trees with trunks four feet in diameter.

As may be judged from some of the common names they bear, such as pigeon plum, fruits produced by a number of South Florida's West Indian trees are an important source of food for wildlife. The wild figs seem to be a favorite with many kinds of birds and, because of this, birds have a supporting role in one of the strangest of natural dramas. The numerous, tiny fig seeds pass undigested through the bird's intestinal tract and begin development where they are dropped. Many plants are distributed in this way, of course, but one of the native figs has the ability to develop equally well whether dropped on the ground or in the crotch of a tree fifty feet above. As the fig seedling grows, some roots may drop directly to the ground and others twine around the host tree while a trunk with a crown of dense foliage grows upward. Eventually, as the roots grow and join, the host is completely enmeshed and killed, and a self-supporting fig tree stands in its place. This strangling habit of growth is employed by a number of trees in the tropical forests, but the strangler fig is the only common practitioner found in South Florida. Trees such as the cabbage palm with its rough trunk, and the live oak, with rough bark and large horizontal limbs, provide particularly favorable spots for strangler fig seedlings. Various stages of the remarkable process can be seen in some of the oaks along Gumbo-limbo Trail.

Visitors viewing the park flora are sometimes disappointed to find so few showy wild flowers. This impression results in part from the fact that most visitors see the area in winter. Plants in South Florida do not regularly have a dormant period imposed by cold weather, but many enter a sort of resting stage during the dry winter months and fewer plants are in flower then than at other seasons. In summer, massed wild flowers sometimes contribute impressive splashes of color to the Everglades landscape. Then aquatic bladderworts may spread a carpet of buttercup-yellow along the flooded

sloughs, marsh pinks enliven the wet prairies, and several kinds of blazing stars lift their tall purple wands of bloom to make a bright haze through the low pinelands.

For most plants the season of flowering is not as brief as is usual farther north, and individual flowers of many interesting and attractive species can be seen nearly any time of the year. Around the freshwater ponds are yellow spatterdock and blue pickerel weed, and the sawgrass glades feature the white stars of the spider lilies and bright scarlet of the swamp milkweed. The pine woods, particularly in areas that have burned not long before, usually offer the most varied floral displays. Among the host of blooms found there is a striking crimson morning glory which is surely one of America's loveliest wild flowers. In open places near the coast the daisy-like flowers of the sea oxeye are commonly seen, and the interesting array of plants adapted to live in salty soil includes a fine blue gentian, a southern representative of a family more frequently associated with cold northern bogs.

Many of the vegetation types of South Florida present particular problems to the growth of smaller terrestrial plants. In the tropical hammocks the floor of the forest is densely shaded most of the time. In the glades and cypress swamps the ground may be flooded for long periods, and the mangrove swamps and some other coastal types, in addition to flooding and deep shade, offer the additional embarrassment of saline

soils. Perhaps the most interesting plants of the region are the ones which have evolved ways out of these difficulties by going, so to speak, upstairs. The vines and air plants, which are so prominent a feature of forest vegetation in the park and throughout the tropics, represent two ways of attaining the higher station essential to survival.

The large number of climbing plants found in the area include many woody and herbaceous vines, and some species which may grow either as trees or vines, depending on individual circumstances. They represent a diverse selection of plants, from vanilla orchids to asters, and show the widest possible variety of structural adaptations for clambering toward the upper strata of the vegetation. A few forms—examples are the green briers, the wild grapes, poison ivy and Virginia creeper—will be familiar to northerners, but many, such as the cruelly armed fishhook vine, or devil's claws, are species of the West Indian tropics. While vines with attractive flowers can be found in all parts of the park, they occur in the greatest abundance and variety in buttonwood hammocks and some mangrove areas near the south coast. Here moonflower vines often blanket the tree tops, especially around forest clearings, and vanilla orchids bear fragrant white flowers on vines that look like stout greenish ropes. Others include several vining milkweeds, a showy white passion flower, and two species of so-called rubber vines related to the cultivated allamanda.

In contrast to the vines, the epiphytes, or air plants, have severed all connections with the ground and gone aloft to form aerial gardens along the trunks and branches of trees. These plants are not parasitic; they utilize their larger neighbors merely for support at a level more favorable for their growth than the shady forest floor. The major kinds of air plants in the park are the orchids and bromeliads.

South Florida has about 25 kinds of epiphytic orchids, ranging in size from tiny ghost orchids to the cow's horn or cigar orchid, large plants, one of which would fill a bushel basket. Several of the species are found only in the Big Cypress Swamp, but many of them occur in the park. As with the tree snails, the beauty and interest of South Florida's epiphytic orchids has contributed to their downfall. For many years, these orchids have attracted great attention from collectors, and, between widespread destruction of their hammock habitats and large-scale commercial collecting, many species have become rare, and some may have been exterminated. While the individual flowers of most of the native orchids are not comparable in size to those of commercially grown varieties, many of them exhibit showy color and attractive form. Some make up for the small size of the flowers by producing a number of tall flower stalks, which may bear 1000 or more blooms. In addition to those which grow as air plants, the park has many terrestrial orchids, including several occurring as common wild flowers of the pinelands and glades.

Bromeliads, representatives of a plant family characteristic of the New World tropics, are the common air plants of the park, where they occur abundantly and in a great variety of shapes and sizes. Most plants of this family grow as epiphytes, but its most renowned member, the cultivated pineapple, is terrestrial. Many of the native forms will also grow in humus on the ground when they happen to be dislodged from loftier sites. The type of bromeliad most commonly seen has a growth form similar to that of the pineapple (they are sometimes called wild pineapples) consisting of a basal rosette of stiff leaves from which a tall flower stalk rises when the plant is mature.

Another type is represented by the well-known Spanish moss, which is much less common in southern Florida than farther north in the southeastern coastal plain. Some of the larger bromeliads are particularly interesting because they catch and store rain water. The leaves are open and spreading above and their bases overlap to form a series of protected cups. A large plant may hold several quarts, and each of these sheltered natural aquaria may support a little world of its own inhabited by various insects, small frogs, lizards, and occasionally even snakes. It has been said that birds and raccoons sometimes depend on bromeliads for their drinking water during periods of very dry weather.

Throughout the park a wide variety of plants, in addition to the orchids and bromeliads, may occur as air plants. They range from tiny liverworts, which grow on leaves in the moist hammocks, to occasional sizable trees which have taken root atop fallen logs. The familiar resurrection fern, with fronds that appear dry and withered during dry spells and turn green again with the first rain, is one of the commonest of air plants. Tropical strap ferns are also common and several other ferns are found almost exclusively as epiphytes on the trunks of cabbage palms. The rich fern flora of the area also includes many terrestrial species. Some grow chiefly on the walls of limestone sink holes while others, such as the giant leather ferns, grow on the ground in hammock sinkholes and along the edges of mangrove swamps.

Cacti, yuccas and agaves, plants more usual in deserts, occur in surprising abundance in coastal areas of the park, especially on beaches and in dry hammocks. Several columnar cacti and the familiar prickly pear also often grow as air plants. One rare species, the mistletoe, or pencil cactus, was an obligate epiphyte in buttonwood forests along the south coast, but it has not been found since hurricane Donna overwhelmed this part of the park in 1960.

*Florida Bay pro-
vides many forms
of recreation.
Canoeists* **ABOVE**
and fishermen
INSET ABOVE
*enjoy sunrise on
the bay.*

CAMEO *Seminole
leader, Billy Bow-
legs.*

MAN

CHAPTER EIGHT

IN THE EVERGLADES

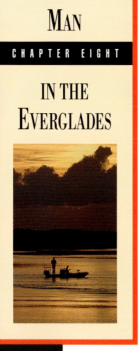

The colorful Indians visitors see along the Tamiami Trail or in the towns of Everglades and Immokalee were not the first to live along South Florida shores or in the hammocks of the remote interior. It is still uncertain when the first Indians arrived. New finds by archaeologists keep pushing the time backward. Perhaps it was as far back as 10,000 years ago.

These first Indians, who may have lived in the region for thousands of years before the coming of the first Europeans, used weapons for hunting. They made fire and cooked with pottery cooking vessels. They made themselves bark shelters and worshipped the gods of nature. They followed the customs of those tribes from the Middle West called "Mound Builders" who erected sand and earth mounds for their temples or as graves for their dead.

The Indians who made their way south to the country of the Everglades liked the climate and found life easy. Great schools of fish swam along the beaches and teemed in the inlets; deer abounded in the pine woods, raccoons and opossums in the jungle-islands. There were clams in reefs and oysters in beds or clustering on the mangrove roots.

The Indians never went back north. They may even have been cut off in the Everglades region by more warlike tribes in northern Florida. For hundreds and hundreds of years they developed in their own way– their villages and mounds everywhere along the rivers and the great lake and outer beaches–in a civilization as unique and strange to the people of the rest of the country as the flat, sun-misted, grass-and-hammock-and-watery Everglades. They had to shape their lives from materials they found in South Florida. They found here no flints for arrow heads and brought in only a few by trade. So they made deadly arrows of hard reeds, sharpened and hardened at the points by fire. The soft Florida limestone was useless for stone picks, hammers and axes. But along the beaches was a wealth of heavy, stone-like shells. With smaller shells they drilled holes in the great pointed whelks so that with deer sinew they could lash them on strong wooden handles for picks and shovels.

The work the Glades Indians did with these shell tools was amazing. They heaped up sand for mounds on which their simple open huts, roofed with durable palmetto, were built above high water. With them they dug out and damned up fish ponds in which they kept live schools of fish and turtles. On remote islands they built sand mounds over the bones of their dead. As time went on, their religion became more complex and the priesthood more demanding. They threw up great series of mounds shaped like bread loaves of half crescents with long earth ramps up which their priests led processions of captives to be burned for sacrifices in the great celebrations to the sun.

There was clay, either gritty or chalky, for pots, but pottery was left to be made by the women and decorated with simple lines or checks. The men, with plenty of time on their hands, indulged in the finest kind of shell and wood carving, for which they found that shark teeth, set in wood handles, were the best possible tools. They carved the columellas of whelk shells with wavy lines as jewelry to hang on long strings from their belts and simpler shapes to serve as net weights. Their finest carving was done of pond apple wood or mangrove wood–small images of gods, fine masks to be worn by dancers in their great processions, wooden plaques carved with shapes

of deer or birds–to indicate the clans of the owners. These were set on long poles about the houses or high on the mounds surmounted with palmetto-thatched temples.

Archaeologists now call this unique Indian civilization the "Glades Indians." Their village sites, their burial mounds, the long canals they dug, bulkheaded with palmetto logs by which they paddled in shelter within the coasts, are not entirely obliterated to this day. We know, from the first Europeans to reach these shores soon after the discovery of the New World, that they were shrewd, independent and warlike. The first Spaniards they ever saw were slavers who had already captured many Bahamian Indians and taken them away to die mining gold in the West Indies. When the slave ships touched South Florida coasts the Glades Indians fought them off with deadly arrows that could penetrate chain mail. Ponce de Leon on his first voyage of discovery had to fight coastal Indians. When, on his second voyage to establish settlements on the lower Gulf Coast he tried to land on a sandy beach in the Ten Thousand Islands, the Indians from behind trees killed some Spaniards and wounded Ponce de Leon himself. He died, defeated, on his way back to Havana.

For three hundred years, as the Spaniards filled North Florida and Georgia with missions and taught their docile Indian converts to cultivate their gardens and attend Mass, the Glades Indians kept their own

country to themselves. From early Spanish writers we know something of the different tribes and villages into which the Glades Indians were divided.

We read about the Matecumbe Indians and the others down the Florida Keys who watched for wrecks of Spanish treasure ships, to salvage iron kettles and hatchets and cloth and gold, and take captive many Spanish men, women and children to be burned in the yearly ceremonials on the high mounds.

Near the Miami River, where, in three centuries, two Spanish missions were started and failed when the Fathers had no more food and presents to give the Indians, the chief and the tribe were known by a name which the Spanish thought was "Tequesta." These East Coast tribes were dominated by powerful tribes who lived on the West Coast about the mouth of the Caloosahatchee and down into the Ten Thousand Islands. Their name sounded to the Spanish like "Calusa." Their chief took tribute and captives from all the other tribes. The gold and treasures from the Spanish ships found their way to him also.

But the Indians cared little for gold or silver or the wonderfully worked jewels the Spanish had stolen from Inca and Aztec temples. The bright metal was too soft to be

Tradi-
tional
costumes of
the late 1800s
adorn the
Indian warriors
PICTURED ABOVE.
Later in the 1900s,
colorful cloth in an ar-
rangement of geometric
forms represented elements in
the environment. Design rows
AT LEFT FROM TOP TO BOTTOM
represent: Bones, Frogs, Rain, Fire,
Crayfish, Turtles, and Horses.

57

worked into useful tools like knives and hatchets so that it was piled carelessly in the Calusa villages for the children to play with. When a powerful Spanish leader, Menendez, made a peaceful visit to Carlos, King of the Calusas, to try to convert him to religion and perhaps slavery, the Spanish soldiers won back much of the treasure by playing for high stakes with the Indians who were always great gamblers. Much of the gold found its way to a quiet tribe of Indians called "Miamis" because they lived on the border of the great lake they called "Miami," now called "Okeechobee." These lake Indians learned most cleverly how to beat out the Spanish gold into plates which they carved with figures of birds and deer to glitter in the sun around the temples on the long poles in place of the wooden plaques. They made fine flat shapes of birds which were used by a burial cult to stick in their ceremonial head bands. These have been found on skulls dug from their burial mounds.

It was a long time, several centuries, after the Spanish first converted the north Florida Indians before the last of the Glades Indians disappeared. They were ravaged by white man's diseases, and there is a legendary account that the remaining few sailed in their canoes to Cuba, away from the crowding white men.

But some of them may have remained in the glades and, mingling with a new migration of Indians from the north, taken part in bloody raids on the settlers beginning to establish their villages on islands off the Everglades coasts.

The breaking up by invading Americans of the country of the Creek Indians of Georgia and Alabama and of the coastal tribes, after the American Revolution, sent scattered groups of Indians pushing down into Spanish Florida, where they were free to live as they chose. One of the earliest of these tribes were the Miccosukee, who first lived in Florida near Tallahassee on a lake bearing their name. With more wars to the north, they moved down the west coast of Florida into the Everglades and the Big Cypress. Their language was that spoken by Indians in Georgia called, "Hitchiti." These were the Indians who may have fought and conquered or married with the last of the Calusas. Some traded with Cuba. Their descendants still live in the Big Cypress and make their camps along the Tamiami Trail.

Once these Indians used to hunt and fish all over the Everglades and the present park. The park displaced only one or two family camps, but it necessarily curtailed their hunting. Ever since the First World War and the building of the Tamiami Trail these still independent Indians, the healthiest in the United States because they live under conditions very like their own chosen natural ones, have made money selling handicrafts

to tourists, picking beans in the vegetable fields and selling hundreds of pounds of froglegs to city markets.

All Florida Indians are loosely called Seminoles, although the name does not designate a particular tribe. Long usage has made it into a sort of surname. Thus the Indians of the Big Cypress and the Tamiami Trail are properly called Miccosukees, while the other large South Florida Indian group are the Cow Creek Seminoles. Each speaks its own language and is somewhat unintelligible to the other though some words are the same.

The Seminole name does not mean "runaway," as has been said, but "people of distant fires." In the days before Florida became an American territory in 1821, a number of Indians from the various tribes of the Creek Confederacy and such coastal people as the Yuchi Indians drifted south into Spanish Florida, escaping before the pressure of American settlers. They were joined there by many escaped slaves from the plantations. They set up their Florida villages on the Alachua Plains, where they had gardens and orange groves and great herds of cattle. They and their Negro companions were free. But owners who wanted to get back their slaves, and Americans who wanted Florida lands, clamored for the United States to buy Florida. In 1821, it was acquired from Spain for five million dollars.

After Florida became a Territory, Commodore David Porter of the U.S. Navy received orders to put down the piracy still troubling the West Indies and American shipping. With his fleet he founded the city of Key West at the end of the Florida Keys. Armed sailboats, under his command, successfully cleaned out the pirates of the Cuban coasts, and American vessels were free to use the great river of the Gulf Stream.

Key Biscayne, which separates the Atlantic from Biscayne Bay, had long been a camping place for slavers, wreckers, pirates and Indians. Now on its tip end was erected Cape Florida Light, the first aid to navigation along that shipwreck-haunted coast.

The great ornithologist, John James Audubon, visited Key West and Indian Key in 1832, the first of a long line of distinguished naturalists to study and describe the wonderful flights of birds, egret and heron and roseate spoonbills now protected in Everglades National Park.

After Florida became a state in 1845, more and more settlers came plodding down by oxcart or horseback from north and west Florida, from Georgia and Alabama. The smoke of their fires rose around the great lake, along the north bank of the Caloosahatchee, along the New River and by the Miami River on Biscayne Bay.

People came over from the Bahamas to Coconut Grove as they already had to the Florida Keys. They began more and more to resent the presence of the peaceful Indians in the Everglades. In 1849 there were wild rumors of white men being murdered by Indians. The Army was sent back to Florida to investigate. The wise old Indian leader Billy Bowlegs brought in the known murderers and turned them over to the white man's justice. But the country was in an uproar, demanding that all the Indians be caught and sent west. The State of Florida deliberately violated its agreement not to permit hunters and surveyors to penetrate the neutral strip between white and Indian lands. The Secretary of War refused to declare war.

People were beginning to think that the Everglades might after all be worth something, if it could be drained. The State called for a regiment of volunteers. A man was hired to catch Indians at so much a head so that they could be sent west. Some soldiers penetrated the Big Cypress and the Turner River and destroyed the garden and banana patch of old Billy Bowlegs. He had done everything he could to keep the peace. Now he went on the war path.

The State of Florida, not the Federal Government, declared war. Both Indians and whites were killed. Houses and camps were burned. The Indians attacked a marching column and killed Lieut. John Parkhill near what is now Collier-Seminole State Park on the Tamiami Trail. The soldiers destroyed camps in the Big Cypress. More people died.

The U.S. Government was anxious to end this disgraceful affair. Billy Bowlegs was paid $6,500, with lesser sums for his warriors, their wives and children, to leave Florida

The Green Corn Dance is the most sacred of all traditions. It is an annual harvest celebration where boys are indoctrinated into manhood, children are given their Indian names, punishment and purification rights are performed and games of skill are played. Stick ball rackets PICTURED ABOVE *are used in playing a lacrosse-like game, men against women. Women prepare months in advance of the celebration sewing the finest of costumes for their families, drying/grinding corn, and collecting medicine plants. Each family group is represented by a matriarchal clan name, like Bird, Otter, Frog, that is passed from mother to child.*

for Indian Territory. They went. It was estimated that about one hundred Indians were left at home in the glades. Actually, there were more than that, but they would never make trouble again. At last, the long miserable war was over.

The Indians increased in their safe haunts, keeping to their ancient ways, governing themselves wisely at the annual Green Corn Dances. When the Civil War came, it did not touch the Everglades or the Indians, except that deserters from both armies found the remote beaches, the open sawgrass and the Ten Thousand Islands–roofed at sunset with thousands of birds–a place where they could live to themselves, and almost as simply as the Indians did. After the Civil War, Key West was a maritime metropolis with a population of more than 5,000. The rest of far southern Florida boasted fewer than half that number, and these widely dispersed along the coast. The interior remained a wilderness with only an occasional Seminole camp to break the solitude.

Change was slow in the decades that followed. Winter farming developed in the Upper Florida Keys and at places on the southern mainland. The chief crops were pineapples, Key limes and vegetables. The first two of these products today have almost disappeared from the agricultural commerce of South Florida. A variety of sportsmen, naturalists and adventurers (and growing numbers of fugitives from northern winters) began to discover the attractions of the area.

So did other fugitives, those seeking a place beyond the reach of the law's long arm. Bit by bit through the last quarter of the nineteenth century the habitable land along the coast came to be sparsely occupied. Some of these settlements have grown into cities; a few, such as Chokoloskee, might still be recognizable to their early settlers; other once-thriving communities, no longer exist. Here and there on the shores and keys of the park one can find signs of some of these lost efforts to coax a living from the fringes of the mangrove swamps–the walls of an old cistern, a date palm or a poinciana tree that shoulders above the invading growth, low ridges marking the pitifully short rows that once were cultivated.

Settlers in the isolated coastal villages and farms lived almost as close to the land as had the Indians before them. Around Miami, some plied the old glades art of making starch from coontie roots. On the lower Gulf Coast many of the towns were built on Calusa shell mounds. Hunting and fishing were important sources of food and livelihood. Events were dated from the years of bad hurricanes. The settlements looked seaward, commonly toward Key West. Small sail boats brought in

mail and supplies and carried out vegetable produce, charcoal, alligator hides, and egret plumes.

Life was hard on this last eastern frontier, and curiosity a trait seldom valued in strangers. The stories of smuggling, moonshine and gun play are legion. Many no doubt have improved in the telling, but some of the goriest tales often turn out to be true. Desperate enterprises and colorful violence, of course, attract attention beyond their real significance.

The history can be told more truly in tamer events: the first school-

house, new boats, new stores, and dreams of eventual development.

Some of the dreams began to be realities and old realities began to fade, as soon as easy land transportation became available. South Florida was at last united with the rest of the nation as modern times marched down the roads and railways along the coasts and into the Everglades with the drainage canals. Development and exploitation at once became the dominant themes. They remain so today.

What succeeded the early times is a story which can be told in terms of epic feats of construction, such as the Overseas Railroad to Key West and the Tamiami Trail, or told as truly in somber episodes of destruction and

Canoes carved from cypress trees provided transportation. Families poled their canoes as far as 70 miles from inland villages ABOVE RIGHT *to trading centers along the coast. Bird and animal skins were traded for cloth, coffee, cooking utensils, sewing machines, and an occasional novelty item like the umbrella* PICTURED LOWER RIGHT *Photographed on the Miami River early 1900s.*

senseless waste. The pioneers came to their task with dredge and bulldozer, and sometimes with more enthusiasm than judgment.

Perhaps most important is the amazing rapidity of the transition. It was 1896 before Miami sprang to life with the arrival of the railroad, and as late as the middle 1920s completion of the Tamiami Trail first gave easy land access between the east and west coasts of southern Florida. The rising tide was checked at times by natural disaster or man's cupidity, but each following wave of development spread farther into the hinterlands. There are still large areas of unsettled wild land, but, except in Everglades National Park and a few other preserves, the days of South Florida's wilderness are numbered, and the number is not large.

Each year new roads and canals divide the remainder into smaller slivers, and the night glow of Miami is seen more brightly from the farthest reaches of the glades. Pine and palmetto, sawgrass and hammock, yield to farms and ranches and close on the heels of the farmers and cattlemen march the subdivisions, the shopping centers, and the used-car lots. The South Florida land at last will be subdued and this conquest will be permanent.

All of this brings us to the park, and its place in regional history. As the tide of development rolled on, there were men who gave thought to preserving a part of South Florida as it was. This counter current had begun before 1900 in the National Audubon Society's long fight to save the plume birds. The conservation movement, often weak and fitful, never lost heart. Everglades National Park is its most notable triumph.

The park can be soundly justified on the basis of its contribution to Florida's booming economy, yet this is not the true reason for its existence. The park might be worth having simply as an exhibit of the raw material from which South Florida was built, a sort of museum where people who live in neat houses on high pineland lots or waterfront lots could come to see a pine tree or observe what a natural shore looks like. That is not the sole purpose, either.

The real reason lies deeper in human consciousness. Everglades National Park, and places like it, exist because we dimly realize that we are yet too close to real frontiers and all of our beginnings to thrive indefinitely in a world of asphalt and concrete. Places of refuge from the hurly-burly still are needed, places where one may escape, if only briefly, all sight and sound of fellow humans.

In ways not simple to explain, American lives are richer because there is still room in the land for crocodiles to build their sandpile nests on the lonely Florida Bay beaches, and for deer to browse in their grace along the willow heads with perhaps a panther to stalk them.